D1555221

THE MANIFESTO OF FREEDOM

Leslie Citron

EAST EUROPEAN MONOGRAPHS, BOULDER
DISTRIBUTED BY COLUMBIA UNIVERSITY PRESS, NEW YORK

1993

EAST EUROPEAN MONOGRAPHS, NO. CCCLVII

Printed in the United States of America

TABLE OF CONTENTS

Foreword   1

Chapter 1   Authoritarian and Statist Aspects of the
             Socialist Doctrine and the Problem of
             Proletarian Inaptitude to Assume the
             Leadership in the Revolution   10

Chapter 2   Proletarian Social Hegemony Under
             the Test of Leninism   25

Chapter 3   The Leninist Concept of the
             "Dictatorship of the Proletariat"   33

Chapter 4   "Socialist" Perspectives Under Stalin   49

Chapter 5   The Illusions Lost   66

Chapter 6   Class Policy Against the Peasantry   78

Chapter 7   The Source of Power:
             Bureaucracy Versus Political Leaders   84

Chapter 8   The Source of Individual Power   92

Chapter 9   Other Alternatives to
             Empirical Socialism   101

Conclusion   Balance Sheet and Conclusions   121
Notes   131
Works Cited   140
Index   144

FOREWORD

A specter is haunting the world–the specter of freedom and democracy. From the plains of Mongolia to the jungles of Nicaragua today the peoples of the world are moving to smash the chains of dictatorship and the bankrupt institutions of empirical socialism.

The ideological tenets of communism have proved in practice to be no more tangible than the existence of afterlife in hell or in heaven.

In the past two decades the socialist societies have undergone a permanent crisis, manifested in all sectors of human activity: social, economic, political, and cultural. The year 1989 was marked by upheaval and change. One after another, the communist governments of Eastern Europe fell, unveiling the deep resentment of the masses toward the economic aspects of socialism. This resentment has manifested itself as much in an eagerness to return to the market forms of economic activity as in the resurgence of religious fervor against the atheist ideological base of communism.

Although the coming changes heralded themselves more than two decades ago, the sudden and wholesale bankruptcy of the socialist political systems came as a surprise for most scholars who specialize in this area. It seems that the sudden conclusion of the Cold War played a major role in laying bare the internal contradictions of socialist economic and political systems.

Although it was previously believed that an arms race of an unprecedented magnitude would have no winners, Western technological achievements, combined with greater financial

1

resources and a more sober economic policy, made the Western allies the clear victors of this contest. Although the Western economies were also strained by the arms race (especially the United States, which came out with a huge public debt) it proved to be catastrophic for the Soviet bloc, which was compelled to radically alter its economic policy and the nature of its politics. All the hidden contradictions and exaggerations of empirical socialism, obscured since 1917 behind a stifling policy of silence, abruptly came to the fore in their naked ugliness.

These unsolved contradictions which intensified problems previously ascribed mainly to capitalism were:

1. An inability to create a workable economic system on the basis of socialist principles.
2. The masses remained aloof to all the experiments of the communist governments designed to improve productivity and to spread the spirit of innovation among the workers.
3. Socialism was unable to create a superior work ethos and socialist societies fell more and more behind the technological revolution experienced in the West.
4. Empirical socialism was unable to end the exploitation of direct producers and concealed this reality behind empty ideological slogans.
5. While the standard of living in the West improved dramatically after World War II, in the Socialist bloc, after seventy years of experimentation, it has shown little improvement and in the end it has come to a dead halt.
6. Nationalism was another unresolved problem. Although Marxism described it as a typical product of the bourgeoisie, it survived the "socialist" revolution and smoldered silently through the years only to burst into violent flames with the failure of socialist economic programs. Ancient animosities not only erupted in Eastern Europe but are menacing the existence of the Soviet Union as well. Helping to intensify these nationalistic feelings were the suppressive policies of Moscow toward the

republic members of the union, especially those on the fringes of the Russian empire. Marx and Lenin's call for "proletarian internationalism" fell on deaf ears when it came to the Russian bureaucrat. Trotsky's international-ist theory of "world revolution" degenerated under Stalin into a pan-slavic dream of world domination.

The actual crisis of the socialist system is due not only to empirical errors in implementing the Marxist ideology, but also to the ideology itself, which has proved in many respects to be unworkable in practice. In the following pages I will attempt to describe the major ideological flaws of Marxism-Leninism.

SETTING THE EQUATION

Six decades have elapsed since the Bolshevik Revolution toppled the Kerensky government, thus inhibiting the hypotheti-cal development of a Western type of democracy in Russia. The Bolshevik coup established its own version of socialism, featur-ing as an essential characteristic the Leninist theory of the dictatorship of the proletariat. After taking political power, the Bolsheviks explained their victorious insurrection as an obvious outcome of historical logic. Inspired by Marxist determinism, Lenin harnessed Marx's earlier predictions concerning the direc-tion of capitalist development toward socialism, in order to justify the Bolshevik bid for power. The last tremors of the armed insurrection were still rumbling when all the parties along the Russian political spectrum, including the socialist parties, came to realize that the general ideas of freedom and opportunity and the particularly socialist ideas of economic equality and mass political power had been nipped in the bud. A subtle but radical Bolshevik political reorientation came to the fore. From this point on, for the short period of their existence, all Russian socialist parties were inadvertently forced into opportunist behavior due to the politico-monopolistic attitude of the Lenin-ists. They came to realize that power was to be appropriated and not extended, monopolized and not shared. Some early Marxists like Plekhanov, Akselrod and Martov had already predicted such an outcome in the early years of the Russian revolutionary movement. Their criticism went beyond Lenin's extremist an exclusivist ideas and touched a major nerve concerning the socialist movement and thought. This was Lenin's interpretation of socialism and its consciousness. The physical separation of the party from the proletariat, and the commanding role of the intellectual-professional revolutionaries in such a party, were products of the Leninist separation of consciousness from the spontaneous movement. Such a situation was considered to be highly at variance with the Marxist theory of class struggle.[1]

Lenin's view that the working class, due to its distinctive economic disadvantages, could not attain socialist conscious-ness by itself and that therefore there was a need for the infusion of such a consciousness from outside, from a professional revolutionary group of intellectual revolutionaries (the party),[2] was considered by socialist critics to be non-Marxist, anti-historical and disdainful of the proletariat.

Although this criticism came from a moral dedication to human welfare and from a quotidian experience in the mass revolutionary movement, in the long run it proved to be idealistic and divorced from the historical reality. Lenin's immediate goal, before the revolution, was to seize political power, a goal that had higher priority than realizing the socialist ideal; consequently, Leninism led to a rejection of a mass party of illiterate workers and was closer to the political reality of the early twentieth century. For such a limited goal as the attainment of political domination, the master-client relationship between party and masses was more conducive to success.

The dissolution of the National Assembly in 1918 was among the first actual signs of the totalitarianism toward which the Bolshevik Revolution was heading. Such an event, if isolated and not repeated time and again, could be considered a historical accident, therefore inconclusive. But the list of infringements on the spirit of democracy is too impressive in the short history of the socialist state. Thirty years later the same scenario was replayed in Eastern Europe and other societies which experimented with socialism.

The vast literature written on socialism in the last century and a half is characterized by a large diversification of antagonistic views. Critics offered many theories and solutions but none suspected, much less described, the peculiar traits which the modern socialist societies are exhibiting at the present time. The Bolsheviks themselves, with all their proneness toward rigidity, when facing the horrendous complexities of establishing a new social order, were time and again compelled to adjust Marxian precepts to historical realities. On other occasions they found themselves in the incongruous role of squeezing the very same reality into the narrow path of Marxian interpretation.[3]

The arbitrariness of the Stalinist era, with its rigidity and intolerance against any experimentation, provided an insurmountable obstacle against any attempt at criticism or revisionism of the Marxist doctrine in order to find a workable alternative to a looming crisis. This crisis, though, found its way to the surface after the death of the dictator, compelling Soviet leaders to undertake the first and hesitant steps toward a partial and marginal liberalization of the system. It was, perhaps, the awkwardness of these attempts, the half-measure solutions and the impotence of the totalitarianism to reform itself, which led given segments of the socialist society to take the initiative and to criticize, first the system, and later the Marxist ideology on which it rested.

At first the Soviet regime enjoyed relative political success due, perhaps, to visionary promises wrapped in enticing plans for greatness and economic development, or perhaps due to the simple outcome of revolutionary inertia triggered by the utter collapse of the tsarist regime. But the new system soon ran out of steam. Years later, the enthusiasm gave way to personal frustration, and hope to disappointment. Despite the relative tolerance shown by some communist regimes, the growing disagreements and criticism, the multitude of problems discussed, and the search for a new methodology of socialist construction, the complex issues of political and economic forms of socialism and the structure of the socialist society are still as much the subject of a heated debate today as they were when the socialism was still in its embryonic form of theoretical speculation.

The Western scholarship did not fare much better. The eagerness for objectivity and for a scientific approach was often marred by partisanship and excessive criticism. The scholars often found imagined faults in socialism rather than the real ones. They were looking more for shortcomings and non-realized Marxist predictions than for the real cause of socialist failure. These shortcomings were often accepted as characteristic of socialism and consequently the entire Marxist ideological complex was dismissed as outdated and inapplicable to the new conditions of the super-technological and post-industrial era.[4]

Inside the socialist movement the number of dissidents was growing rapidly. Beside the oldtimers like Grigorii Rakowsky, James Burnham, and Milovan Djilas, a whole generation of young critics conditioned in the caldrons of communist education were directing their political sting toward the theoretical fabric of socialism. These critics cover a broad spectrum, from the hardcore Marxists to those who have completely abandoned the Marxist ideology and relinquished any hope for a meaningful redemption of the socialist system. As Djilas pointed out:

> The communists are chiefly to blame for their own misfortunes. The result of their obstinacy in pursuing an imaginary society, in the belief that they could change human nature, is that their ideas and they themselves have been inexorably crunched by the frenzy of the violence they perpetrated. The human being under communism, as in all situations at all times in human history, has proved intractable and quite unfit for any ideal models, particularly those that seek to restrict his boundaries and prescribe his destiny.[5]

Other critics, less pessimistic, are looking for answers either in the revision of the old Marxist ideology or in finding new ways and theories to explain what really happened in the first half of the twentieth century and where these developments will lead.

These ideological rejections, clashes, and compromises, along with an overall soul searching, indicate that something was or went wrong with socialism. Given the relatively short time since the inception of empirical socialism and the magnitude of the problems that have evolved since then, one cannot avoid the stern fact that at least in part, Marxism is inapplicable, that the man for whose deliverance Marxism supposedly was created is not or never will be mature enough, or for that matter, naive enough, to accept and totally submit to it.

Since the inception of the socialist state in Russia and later in the countries of Eastern Europe, an increasing number of leading analysts have been questioning the real nature of the so-called socialist societies. The common citizens of these countries also sensed that something was missing in the makeup of their society, that an ever-increasing gap existed between official statements and propaganda and the reality in which they lived. This grass-root disenchantment with reality manifested itself violently as early as the Kronstadt rebellion. It remained quite diffuse and impulsive, though, without being able to elevate itself to the level of a scientific analysis of the new social conditions that were being formed. The scrutiny of the stark reality was done first by the disenchanted leaders of the revolution, epitomized by Trotsky, who felt it to be their duty to criticize a system which departed from their expectations and, one may say, personal interests. Later, such criticism was attempted even by some communist leaders who still enjoyed the privileges in which their class fellows indulged themselves, but were either forced by adverse circumstances or driven by moral considerations to take an oppositionist stance. The latter manifestations of criticism are today merging with a larger current of disenchantment found mostly among intellectuals who did not find their place in the new social order.

Finally, the most obvious critics of the new social conditions should be mentioned, those Western scholars who lived outside the geographical area of the socialist states and in a more or less objective manner questioned the nature of East European socialism from its beginnings to the present time. These new conditions offer fertile ground for research by allowing analytical inquiry into the real nature of "socialist" societies.

The present work attempts to fathom the different theories and opinions concerning the nature of socialism and to juxtapose them to the historical reality from which they emerged. But this effort alone cannot cover the whole problem. Along with the fact that many facets of Marxism were rendered obsolete by successive historical developments, there were intrinsic parts of Marxism that were impossible to apply even at the time when the foundations of Marxism were first laid down. Subsequent developments not only confirmed this statement but brought into doubt they very possibility that these aspects of Marxism could ever be applicable to a realistic plan of building a society with socialist characteristics. These Marxian components are the following:

1.   Elements of totalitarianism expressed by the increasing role of the state in controlling every facet of social activity, extending well beyond the initial period of transformation. Conversely, as predicted by Marxism, the state would wither away and disappear soon after the socialist revolution.

2.   The dictatorship of the proletariat as an instrument of repression in the hands of the proletariat.

3.   The leading role of the proletariat in the socialist revolution and socialist construction.

4.   The political coalition between the industrial workers and peasantry in the process of socialist edification. A coalition based on the convergence of their economic and social interests.

These are the elements of the ideology which deviated the most from the Marxist doctrine as envisioned by Marx and Engels. The aim of this analysis is to demonstrate that the application of these ideological tenets will produce almost identical results anywhere, in every situation regardless of economic or social matrix, even in the absence of Soviet–style pressures toward economic and political conformism.

Parts of this book were written well before the political events of 1989 in Eastern Europe. Many of its predictions came through during those events. The rest is up to history to decide.

L. C.

THE IDEOLOGY

CHAPTER I

Authoritarian and Statist Aspects of the Socialist Doctrine and the Problem of Proletarian Inaptitude to Assume the Leadership in the Revolution

The incipient ideas of socialism are almost as old as the history of mankind. From the beginning, it may be said, socialist ideas were not the exclusive product of some sensitive minds concerned with human destiny, nor a direct reflection of deteriorated social relations, although the deterioration of a traditional social equilibrium might influence the frequency and impact of socialist ideas and encourage a spurt of socialist models offered as a cure for those social ailments. Furthermore, the similar concept that the number and intensity of socialist doctrines are in direct proportion to the degree of social injustice experienced during a given historical period is not fully demonstrated historically. What is obvious, though, is that the most incipient and primitive socialist ideas already contained authoritarian elements calling for one or more social institutions or authorities to be placed above the society in order to fulfill the ideological vision of social justice.

Less commented upon and less emphasized but present in almost all socialist writing, excepting the anarchists, is the idea of using authority as an instrument to influence different facets of social life for the supreme benefit of socialism. Later this idea of authority, personified in the state, was utilized more specifically in Marxian socialism as an instrument to modify economic relations and to plan, supervise, and lead social production toward the eradication of private property and social inequality.

This recurring idea of authority, understood as state authority, far from being abandoned as a hindrance to socialist freedom, is continuously mentioned in various socialist programs. This idea is already existent in Thomas More's *Utopia,* where the organization of social production is assigned to the state.[1] It is manifest in the works of the late eighteenth- and nineteenth-century utopians side by side with their reformist, moral, religious or other normative concepts. It appears nebulously in the writing of Owen and Weitling, but is more defined in Saint Simon, where he abandons economic liberalism and formulates the principle of a "future 'organic' social community."[2] He assigns to the state a major role in allocating investment credits and other means of production to manufacturers in accordance with their abilities and social needs, and calls for the state to supervise the rights to use the means of production.[3] The same theme is expressed by Proudhon's theory of state as a means to organize social production, despite his earlier rejection of this theory as a communist way of securing political monopoly through the institutions of an omnipotent state.[4] Blanc also expressed his hopes that a "gradual reform by the state would abolish inequality, exploitation, crisis and unemployment."[5] The role of the state as a social modifier already loomed strong during the French Revolution when the Babouvist movement departed from the main direction and goals of the bourgeois revolution, choosing its more radical course of economic expropriation under the auspices of a state of paupers. Here Kolakowski melancholically notes that the Babouvist movement constituted the watershed at which liberal democracy and communism began to part company. Here "it came to be seen that equality was not a completion of liberty, but a limitation of it."[6]

As already mentioned, the idea that state authority as an equalizing force over society and the economy is not only necessary but constitutes the only avenue to achieving socialism, both socioeconomically and psychoculturally, was fulfilled in the empirical strivings of the Russian Marxists after the Bolshevik revolution.

Other, more minute elements of this theory, like economic planning, socialist *weltanschauung,* the empirical forms of workers' self-management, are only later expressions of the same concept. In time, with the development of the socialist idea the concept of state authority grew and was connected by Marxism to the historical rise of the proletariat, which would perform the task of social leader through the function of the dictatorship of the proletariat.

Marx, borrowing from Hegel's philosophical interpretations, was searching for the objective inner force which moves history ahead and which in Hegelian terms was the principle behind the logic of conflict, self-contradiction, and strife. As Lichtheim stated, for Marx "The self-activating principle must be discovered within the historical process itself, and so far as modern society was concerned Marx in 1844-45 believed he had located the unconscious agent of transformation: it was the proletariat."[7]

From this inadvertently comes the conclusion that the driving force in social development must not be a conscious one, especially in the early period of its development. After all, the bourgeoisie itself was not conscious of the final political results of its economic activity, that it would replace as a social hegemon the feudal landlords that it served so faithfully in financial and commercial matters. By the same token neither must the proletariat be, at the beginning, conscious of its historical role as the gravedigger of capitalism. The proletariat will have all the time it needs to mature during the socialist revolution.

At this point, though, we reach an unsolved conjuncture. If the crisis of capitalism is the direct cause of the socialist revolution, which class will become the leader of that revolution and why? What are those characteristics which determine the hegemonic role of a particular class? Marxism points to the bourgeoisie as the hegemonic element in the destructive process of feudalism. Marx and Engel's statements are well known on this subject:

> The bourgeoisie, wherever it has got the upper hand, has put an end to all feudal, patriarchal, idyllic relations. It has pitilessly torn asunder the motley ties that bound man to his 'natural superiors'....The bourgeoisie has stripped of its halo every occupation hitherto honoured and looked up to with reverent awe. It has converted the physician, the lawyer, the priest, the poet, the man of science, into paid wage labourers....The bourgeoisie cannot exist without constantly revolutionizing the instruments of production, and thereby the relations of production; and with them the whole relations of society....The bourgeoisie, during its rule of scarce one hundred years, has created more massive and more colossal productive forces than have all preceding generations together.[8]

Marx has emphasized that among the many social strata coexisting in the feudal system only the bankers and merchants represented that occupational group which has formed the economic core of capitalism. In contrast, Marxism fails to pinpoint that specific occupational characteristic which would put the industrial worker on the first line of social hegemony. While the bourgeoisie developed inside the feudal system, as the proletariat did later in capitalism, it was not really a product of the medieval economy and not a coherent part of it. The capitalist economy evolved on the periphery of the feudal economy and only later did it penetrate and prevail over it. From the beginning the bourgeoisie exhibited its basic features as an independent, diversified, and entrepreneurial class. Conversely, the proletariat is described by Marx and Engels as a direct product of the capitalist system and an integral part of it. It seems that they nurtured no special illusions and expressed many contradictory views about them. They describe the proletariat either as a downtrodden class of industrial helots or as the future leading class whose triumph over capitalism is linked to the attainment of socialism.[9]

Under capitalist conditions, according to Marx, the worker has to sell his labor power in order to survive, and this happens in the midst of a process which turns labor into a commodity.[10] In the Communist Manifesto he and Engels describe the worker as an appendage of the machine a creation of the capitalist economy which develops proportionately with the development of the bourgeoisie, and its capital. They refer to "a class of labourers, who live only so log as they find work, an who find work only so long as their labour increases capital."[11] They also point to the monotony of industrial work, the minimal creative and intellectual involvement, the workers' loss of individuality and their alienation from the productive process and from the society in which they live. All this happens in a process in which "they are daily and hourly enslaved by the machine, by the overseer, and above all, by the individual bourgeois manufacturer himself."[12]

This description hardly squares with the tremendous historical purpose assigned to the workers by Marxism. Here we should consider not only the physical and economic deprivation of the workers, much emphasized by Marxism, which renders impossible their elevation to the rank of social hegemon, especially in the short period of time allocated to them, but also the intrinsic character of industrial workers as a class of executors.

Previously I quoted Marx and Engels where they emphasize the dependency of the worker on capital, and a look at the history of the workers' movement will confirm this dependency. Industrial workers never acted as an independent class, with its own innovative goals aimed at a radical change of the social structure. All the innovative schemes calling for structural changes, including Marxism, were devised by radical intellectuals. Unlike the bourgeoisie, the workers never challenged the various social classes, including their own, to clear away obstacles in the path of industrial development.[13] The workers never dominated the production forces but were always only a part of these forces. They never represented a mode of production but always were represented by that mode of production. In fact there have been many instances when the immediate interests of the workers, or what they thought to be their interests, were contradictory to the smooth operation of production. From the Luddite movement in England to the protests of the Polish workers in the early 1980s there has been a long series of strikes, rebellions, and protests; although these were in most cases legitimate, nevertheless they hindered the smooth development of the economy. This is to show that social justice does not always go hand in hand with economic progress.

As we will see later on, there always was a distinction between a true workers' movement, mainly aimed at their economic betterment, and an ideology and program of political behavior injected from the outside, which workers never actually accepted as their own. The propagandistic pressure coming from different communist parties, and the temporary attachment of the worker's movement to communist political actions may have given the impression of identity of goals. This supposed identity of goals, emphasized by communists from Marx and Engels[14] to the present ideologues, does not withstand the scrutiny of a close analysis. True, there were many instances when workers participated in political actions from the revolutions of 1848 to the "Socialist Revolution" in Russia, but by the same token there are countless instances of workers' participation in, and full support for, such "bourgeois" political tendencies as nationalism and wars. It rather seems that the dislocating force of the strikes, slowdowns, rebellions, etc., with which the workers' movement is equipped, was used by different political movements as the muscle power to further their own causes, which they represented as the interest of the popular masses. Transforming the workers' organization into a class and later into a political party is made difficult–as Marxism itself stresses–by the fact that despite their identical economic interests, workers' unity is broken up, now and then, by individual competition between the workers.[15] This political unreliability exhibited by workers seems to demonstrate that the workers' movement has less influence on events than events have on the workers' movement. Marx and Engels themselves pointed out that the fluctuating composition of the industrial workers' class, where the rank and file is daily augmented by ruined middle class and peasant elements[16] is continually exposed to foreign ideologies. Later, many of Lenin's writings commented on the same phenomenon: the workers' tendency to accept unproletarian views and ideologies. These observations lead inevitably to the question: how can one entrust the social hegemony into the hands of a heterogeneous, ideologically fluctuating class whose goals never actually reach beyond immediate economic goals and whose activity, directed to the construction of a new society, never pass beyond the level of the barricades? The truth is that nobody, including the communists, ever entrusted such stewardship to the industrial working class.

In the last analysis it was expected that the state would accomplish by coercion what the proletariat was unable to accomplish by means of democracy. The question of state, its origin, and purpose was debated extensively inside and outside the Marxist framework. It is too complex an issue to deal with in a detailed fashion here.

In the Marxist ideology, despite the great variations of forms in which it has appeared in history, the state is considered a complex machinery controlled by the owners of the means of production in order to subdue and control the producers of material and intellectual goods. In other words the state as an instrument of coercion in defense of class interest presupposes at least the elements of a class division.[17] This contention was refuted by many political scientists and sociologists, while others gave some credence to it.

The survival, after the socialist revolution, of the coercive features of the state together with its social stabilizing functions was explained away as a result of the temporary survival of the exploiters and with the apologetic reasoning that the state in this period serves the majority anyway. This period of transition, when supposedly the majority coerces the minority, was called the period of the dictatorship of the proletariat.

On the issue of the dictatorship of the proletariat Marxist ideology is no more elucidative than on the previous issues. It starts from the premise that when political power has been won by the proletariat its "historical mission" is by no means ended. A given social setup cannot be changed into a radically different one overnight. The proletariat, once in power, must gradually dissolve the capitalist economic mechanism and its political and social institutions and replace them with the organs of the new order. In this way the period of the dictatorship of the proletariat is considered, by Marxist ideologues, to be a unique period of history when deep social, economic, and psychological transformations occur under the conditions that arise when first, political power is won and is followed only later by economic supremacy. As Bober pointed out: "Marx and Engels maintain that political authority is indispensable during the period in which society is being transformed into a socialist commonwealth."[18] This political authority is to be personified by the proletarian state, which will perform most of the tasks set up by the demands of the dictatorship of the proletariat.

If the institution of a proletarian state purporting to represent proletarian interests is clearly described by Marxists, the detailed process of creating such a state is much less so. Does Marxism envision a simple change of personnel, formed by proletarian elements inside the old state institutions, or the change of these institutions, too, along with their structure and aim? What made Marxists assume that the elected officials, notwithstanding their proletarian origin, would remain dedicated to the old proletarian principles and not form a new coalition of interest, a coalition of those who control the levers of power? Perhaps Marx and Engels expected the democratic essence of this dictatorship to prevail. The actual historical experience, though, contradicted these expectations, because neither did the leaders remain faithful to the class they came from, nor did the state institutions really change their profile and character. Apart from minor cosmetic changes the state has maintained the same, or even accentuated, oppressive structure and it is aimed in the same direction: against the majority of the population.

This conclusion is reinforced by a remark by Marx himself in his address to the General Council of the International Workingmen's Association: "The Commune furnished in particular the proof that the working class is not in condition simply to take over the existing political mechanism and put it into operation for its own use."[19]

It seems that Marx and later Lenin attributed this to the insufficient ideological development of the proletariat, although the most recent events point to the fact that there are deeper social and economic issues which prohibit the hegemony of the proletariat and the democratization of the "socialist" governments.

According to Marxism, after the dictatorship of the proletariat has done its historical task communism becomes a reality. This reality is accomplished either in two or three phases depending on from which period the countdown for communism started. Thus taking an early period of communist transformation we encounter a first phase of radical transformation in which capitalist institutions gradually are replaced by the socialist ones. In this period coexistence between the two types of institutions is quite common. In other words the advance of socialism is spread evenly over the different fronts of social activity.

The second phase is socialism itself, which Marx termed as the first phase of communism. In this period there are still some remnants of classes but no exploitation; work becomes a social and moral obligation, yet distribution still exhibits capitalist features; and production will first cover social needs with the rest to be divided according to work performed.[20] The third phase is complete when communist concepts dominate every facet of public and private life. There are no classes and no exploitation. A new generation of man appears which experiences no traces of capitalism either in its economy or in its mental processes. The state has vanished, and as Engels pointed out: "The government of persons is replaced by the administration of things." Now social concerns dominate the individualist approach.

> It is a society worthy of human nature. The contradictions of the old order are gone. Gone at last is the mastery of man over man. Society pools its assets in labor, natural wealth, capital and science; calculates the diverse needs of its members; and apportions the resources among the multiple industrial channels, to insure an uninterrupted and rich flow of products for every want. Coordinate with social production is social enjoyment of the income. After the necessary deductions for public purposes, the social storehouse is shared by all, not according to their contribution, but in the light of a principle transcending the capitalist idea of equitable distribution. Emblazoned on the flag of communism is the motto: 'From each according to his capacity, to each according to this need.'[21]

It seems that for Engels this is the apex and the last link in the chain of transformations through which the mode of production must pass. As again Bober points out: "This final mode of production proclaims 'the ascent of man from the kingdom of necessity to the kingdom of freedom'."[22] But can one imagine the continuous further development of economic institutions without its due reflection in social relations? Does this not mean the negation of Marxism by Marxism? If one accepts the Marxist formula of social relations as a reflection of economic conditions then the future obsolescence of the communist system must appear to have the force of a natural law. But we do not have to go so far in history to find utopia in the Marxist ideological structure. Kolakowski points out that:

> Marx's socialist programme did not involve the extinction of individuality or a general leveling for the sake of the 'universal good,' a conception of socialism characteristic of many primitive communist doctrines....To Marx socialism represented the full emancipation of the individual by the destruction of the web of mystification which turned community life into a world of estrangement presided over by an

alienated bureaucracy...what Marx desired to see was a community in which the sources of antagonism among individuals were done away with.[23]

But where to find that force which will emancipate the individual worker enchained in the double oppression of capitalist exploitation and the petty and narrow tyranny of the economic interests of his own class? Will it be the revolutionary intellectual who decides to put an end to capitalism by using the insurrectionary power of the proletariat? As history has demonstrated, they were able to direct a blow at capitalism but completely unable to free either the individual worker or the proletarians as a class from the characteristics and economic functions they inherited from capitalism. In other words what the revolutionary intellectual was able to accomplish was to get rid of the "alienated bureaucracy," after describing a whole circle of "socialist" revolution, only to replace that alienated bureaucracy with another similar one.

The way in which Marx developed his concepts on socialism was to take the major characteristics of the capitalist system, turn them inside out and create a reverse image of that society in which all negative aspects of the old were transformed into the positive aspects of the new.

The concept of modern socialism, as developed by Marx, was intended to be not only a solution to the problem of alienated labor but also a logical outcome to the conclusions reached by Marx in his analysis of the capitalist system and concerning the direction of capitalist development.

According to Marx, capitalism, like any social order in history, experiences two phases, the expanding and the declining phases. During the expanding phase the productive forces experience rapid progress, and the maladies that reflect the structural shortcomings of capitalism, such as poverty, underconsumption, the falling rate of profit, and periodic crises, do not yet assume threatening proportions and have little impact on the working classes, who have not yet attained class consciousness. When capitalism has reached the stage of maturity and decline, as it had in 1848, the contradictions become more evident and disruptive.[24]

> Daily the capitalist class demonstrates its incapacity to perform the functions it assumed. 'It is unfit to rule,' cries the Communist Manifesto, 'because it is incompetent to assure an existence to its slave within his slavery.' It cannot maintain an uninterrupted increase of capital and a steady development of the productive forces, and periodically it rocks the economy with convulsions and breakdowns. The 'historical task and privilege' of the capitalist class is to foster the productive forces to a state in which they can serve as the elements of a higher order. Such a task it has already achieved, an it is incapable of making further use of them.[25]
>
> As the capitalist system contains the seeds of its own destruction, so it harbors ingredients which will go into the composition of the new system. This refers not only to the productive forces which the future society will take over but to intimations within the capitalist organization of the context into which the productive forces will be placed under socialism.
>
> These intimations find their expression in the joint-stock company with its 'social capital,' social because it is supplied by multitudes of investors and because it represents a 'social enterprise,' and the cooperative establishments, where 'associated laborers' plan their work without the benefit of the obsolescent capitalist.[26]

These particular Marxist assessments are inconclusive. Never in history has an economic system experienced a smooth, uninterrupted development safe from one or another type of crisis. In ancient times the low productivity of slave work caused continuous economic problems, especially in the later stages of the period, when there was an expanding state and increased consumption. Falling productivity had to be compensated for with a large number of slaves, a phenomenon conducive to continuous wars for spoil. In the Middle Ages the system of land and title inheritance, the first-born male inheriting both, collided by the eleventh century with the reality of a growing number of aristocrats and a diminishing amount of land to be apportioned among them. This created the acute necessity for an eastward expansion, carried out mainly through the phenomenon of the Crusades. Furthermore, the growing agricultural output in the later centuries of the Middle Ages, the quantitative increase of merchandise, both agricultural and handcrafted, collided with an acute shortage of money, and the gold imported from the newly discovered Americas produced deep social and economic dislocations. While it is true that these systems lasted for a long time and were much more stable economic structures than capitalism, it should not be forgotten that these were mostly closed economies which were based mainly on community production and consumption and were very slow in the development of productive forces.

The advances in sciences and technology, the geographical discoveries, and the influx of gold and raw materials boosted production to levels unknown in earlier periods of history. But these advances were mainly due to outside resources. To achieve its full potential of economic development, society needed the complete liberation of the entrepreneur from all the fetters and shackles of interdependence and collective responsibility which characterized feudalism. The individual needed to be free to act on behalf of his own interests. But liberation of the individual meant the appearance of thousands of creative, free-lance agents competing for the same objective, the one that assured continuous growth: profit. Social progress was achieved through the progress and success of each particular agent, acting independently. Capitalism created an odd situation: the increased collectivism in production was matched with the increased independence and individualism of the entrepreneur. It would be possible to discuss endlessly the correctness of such a process if the whole issue were not an exercise in futility. Unfortunately, in the overwhelming majority of the cases, the historical processes were not a product of normative beliefs but the outcome of objective needs achieved in the cheapest and most convenient way for the entrepreneurs. In this case the way was the destruction of the intricate and complex feudal relations that determined the collective responsibilities of the social leaders, in their position of suzerainty, and of the peasants, who were collectively responsible to the landlords. But the burst of individualism and creativity so characteristic of the first stages of the capitalist system carried with it the other, negative, side of the coin. Under capitalism, financial resources and creativity, the major components of capitalist success, are provided by individuals each pursuing his own interests. The result is an economic structure that changes an adapts in order to accommodate to the system's need for mass investment. Such investment is achieved either in a capitalist way through joint-stock companies, cooperatives, and giant multinational companies, or the socialist way, in which the state becomes the focal point of forced mass financial accumulations and investments. A negative aspect of capitalism, of course, was the waste of human and material resources through the wild competitive scramble among the producers. But this was, it seems, the only practical way to act at this stage of capitalist development, in order to break away from the slumbering collective responsibility of the feudal system. Although not the most ethical, it was the easiest way to harness the surfacing economic potentialities.

It was a matter of choosing between a dormant and relatively stable feudal system or a dynamic and creative, albeit insecure, capitalist system. As we know, history opted for progress and not for normative morality. As for the Marxist assessment that breakdowns in the capitalist economy become more and more common and more widespread, engulfing all aspects of the economic and social life and driving capitalism to its demise, it appears, again, to be unsubstantiated. Not that anybody would deny the increasing size of these economic recessions but these powerful shocks can be attributed to the increased size of the economy and its omnipresence in all facets of human activity. There is nothing to indicate that these crises mean the immediate end of the capitalist system. Perhaps other forms of economic organization and other ways to approach social production will be necessary but to confuse adjustment with finality is conducive to nothing but confusion.

To these shortcomings in the ideological content of Marxism must be added those of a psychological and methodological nature. Although Marx and Engels made visible efforts to preserve a detached, analytic, and objective approach to the issues involved, their activity in the politics of the workers' movement, the emotive aspect of such involvement, the number of issues thus encountered, and the instinctive desire for quick and radical solutions had a negative influence on their economic and social analysis. Forced time and again to adapt their theories to the ad hoc requirements of the workers' movement, they came to superficial conclusions on the political realities, especially on issues such as the political future of the proletariat and that of socialism itself. It would be wrong to consider this departure of Marxism from objectivity as due only to bias. The methodological limitations of the social science and lack of sufficient data doomed Marxism to the fate of previous social theories, namely an inability to anticipate and to solve the complexities of future social development. The solutions given by Marxism to these problems remained similar to the previous theories, which took a moral-normative approach to such issues. In other words Marxism, like the earlier theories, continued to feature a large body of utopian thinking.

CHAPTER II

Proletarian Social Hegemony Under the Test of Leninism

In a subsequent historical epoch, more precisely in 1917, when the revolution became reality and the Bolsheviks, through iron discipline and a ruthless policy, managed to secure a monopoly of political power for themselves, the very fact of their political success imposed a tremendous burden on the new leaders. For want of any historical, juridical, or representational justification they tried to defend their monopoly of power as a historical necessity to prepare the stage for a proletarian social and political hegemony. Marxist doctrine, with its prognosis of unavoidable capitalist development toward socialism, and Lenin's addition of the possibility, and even the necessity, of building socialism in one country, proved very useful to this attempt. For this reason the defense of the ideological purity of Marxism against any type of challenge or revision, whether from left or right, became the main obsession of the Bolshevik leaders. The practical outcomes of this attitude was the ideological rigidity and political stagnation which enveloped the Bolshevik party in the post-revolutionary era.

Despite his staunch support of Marxian tenets, it seems that Lenin may already have had serious doubts, in his early years of political activity, concerning the role of the proletariat in the revolution and the construction of socialism. These doubts came to the surface in several of his statements in which he indirectly questions the ability of the proletarian class to make programmatic political judgements and to assume social leadership. The

25

source of his doubts can be found in the Marxian assessment of the industrial proletariat and in the historical development of this class.

According to this Marxian assessment, during the nineteenth century the physical laborers engaged in industrial activity were viewed strictly as a "proletariat" with potentialities for social leadership while mental labor remained the preserve of the ruling class.[1] At that time it was expected that the number of industrial workers would increase and eventually constitute the majority of the population. As long as the first stage of the industrialization process lasted in Europe and North America, the number of industrial workers increased spectacularly, although without becoming the majority of the population. The consequences of this growth was an increasing anxiety on the part of the Marxian theorists, especially Lenin, who feared the "dangers" of "outside" ideological influences on the "proletariat due to the large number of ruined small proprietors" who joined the ranks of the proletariat. This anxiety was undoubtedly based on the realization that the proletariat, lacking any ideology of its own and especially lacking any real possibility of creating one, could become an easy prey to the ideological influences and interests of other classes prepared to assume the social leadership. Later, with the introduction of a more complex technology in the productive process, this situation became more evident and the increased role of highly qualified workers and technical personnel forced Lenin to recognize that changes in production technology affected the very structure of the proletariat as a class. He acknowledged the existence of an increasing gap between qualified workers, whose educational advantages enabled them to play a role in the complex operations assigned, and the rest of the mass proletariat.[2]

This historical reality of the industrial proletariat with its heterogeneous composition and the economic-cultural backwardness of its majority, compelled Lenin to write in December 1919:

Only the illusion of petty-bourgeois democrats, of socialist and social-democrats and their most prominent leaders can create the belief that under the capitalist regime the mass of workers can attain a sufficient degree of consciousness, firmness of character, insight and breadth of political outlook to decide solely by means of vote, or decide by any means at all, except after a long experience of class war, to follow definitely any given party....

Capitalism would not be capitalism if it did not...condemn the masses to brutishness, timidity, diffuseness and ignorance.[3]

In several other works Lenin acknowledged the inability of the working class to develop its own ideology, for reasons explained above. While Lenin recognized this fact, he emphatically assigned to this impediment a transitory character. For this reason he emphasized the decisive influence of the radical intelligentsia, as a means not only of neutralizing the impact of bourgeois ideology, but also of revolutionizing the working masses caught up in the momentum of the spontaneous movement.[4]

Lenin's recognition that workers' mentality has developed spontaneously and is liable to be influenced both by socialist and bourgeois ideology, inadvertently leads to the conclusion that the industrial working class lacked, and subsequent historical development has proved that it still lacks, those basic characteristics which make a social class the leader of its historical time.

Although Lenin didn't expect the immanency of a Russian uprising (the February revolution was a surprise for him, too) the increasing social tensions in Russia, intensified by the rigors of war, and the lack of a realistic plan for the construction of socialism, compelled him to launch a program in which the objective was to resolve the social and economic crisis by immediately implementing the political methodology called the dictatorship of the proletariat. Some of his ideas, such as the expropriation of the proprietor classes and the dictatorship of the proletariat had already been expressed in the early period of the Marxist movement, but in the period immediately before, during, and after the Russian Revolution, these political concepts were augmented with new ones. Some of these, such as the policy to be taken toward the peasant during the dictatorship of the proletariat, the emphasis on "centralism" in the Communist Party and the Soviet state, the postponement of the "withering away of the state," became primary concerns, overshadowing everything else. In this way the building of a socialist society was divided into two periods, with the first dealing with those immediate issues that had brought about the Russian political and social crisis. This first step was presented as an introduction to socialism. Issues such as expropriation of land and industry, the reinforcement of the state, and even the drastic measures of "war communism," were considered as the first step toward the new egalitarian society, nonexistent until that time in the history of civilization. By concentrating on a program extending only to the ad hoc issues, and dealing with the crisis of Russian society, instead of attempting to assess the implementability of a still highly theoretical socialism, Lenin gave himself a respite in which to determine the direction which the proletariat was going to take in its political maturation and its eventual emergence as a conscious political force capable of social hegemony. In this way the dictatorship of the proletariat came to be considered as a historical necessity, with the mission of carrying out the processes of an entire historical period, which Marxism identified as the first stage of socialism. Kolakowski pointed out very well that the whole complex issue of socialist transformation was reduced to "the confiscation of bourgeois property," and that "all manifestations of discontent are relics of the bourgeois past and should be treated accordingly."[5]

Later, confronted with growing problems and actually unable to show any real economic and social progress which could be defined as uniquely socialistic, Lenin had to concede that the Bolsheviks were not out to "introduce" socialism immediately, but to create "favorable" conditions for the building of the socialist society.[6]

> We must bear in mind [Lenin wrote] that we have never set ourselves 'insoluble' social problems, and as for the perfectly soluble problem of

taking immediate steps toward socialism, which is the only way out of the exceedingly difficult situation, that will be solved only by the dictatorship of the proletariat and poor peasants.[7]

This ideological hesitation concerning the implementation of socialism became even more evident when, overwhelmed by economic difficulties, the Bolsheviks were forced in 1921 to retreat to the capitalist economic methodology of the New Economic Period (NEP).

Lenin, in his analysis of twentieth century capitalism, starts from the Marxist concept that capitalist development will lead to the increasing concentration and centralization of capital, punctuated by intermittent economic recessions and ending, in Lenin's opinion, in a comprehensive and devastating economic crisis that will create a general crisis of the capitalist system.[8] When this Leninist theory is compared with his limited expectations from empirical socialism and his hesitations concerning the ideological potentialities of the proletariat, one is bound to doubt its validity. Such a theory could be accepted if it included some major components of a radical social and economic change. Such a component would obviously be the existence of a new dynamic class, with entrepreneurial and hegemonic capabilities able to lead the entire society to a partial or radical, sudden or gradual change–a class which would be able to demonstrate its leadership qualities in all areas of social activity, such as production, technology, science, and culture. It is also imperative to take into account other components of this equation, such as social traumas (wars, famine, a breakdown in production, etc.), which could trigger the already existent tensions into a full explosion. In this case the absence of the first condition renders Lenin's theory of the transitional character of monopolist capitalism and of the dictatorship of the proletarian class null. To put this another way: Lenin predicted the immanency and inevitability of a socialist revolution, carried out under the leadership of an industrial proletariat whose ideological potentiality is limited, and which, therefore, must surrender the political power, at least temporarily, to a communist vanguard recruited from the revolutionary intelligentsia, which presumably is capable of leading, and which, in turn, will return power to the proletariat when they have reached political maturity. It sounded plausible, but unfortunately history did not confirm this theory. Lenin's ambiguity in mixing the concept of communist intelligentsia with that of the proletariat and presenting the intelligentsia as a vanguard of the working class was already extant in his early works concerning the organizational structure of the Bolshevik Party. This ambiguity was reemphasized during World War I in such works as "Imperialism the Highest Stage of Capitalism" and "The Task of the Proletariat in the Present Revolution."[9]

In the first of the above-mentioned books, Lenin concludes that the development of monopoly capitalism from free competitive capitalism is "the transition from the capitalist system to a higher socio-economic order"[10] [socialism]. In putting forward this theory of transitionalism, Lenin fails to demonstrate why this "higher" socio-economic system must and will be socialist and not, for that matter, a third, higher phase of the already existent capitalism. Lenin's argument that the phenomena accompanying monopoly capitalism, such as a high concentration of capital (through cartels, trusts, associations, etc.); the seizure and continuous dividing up of colonies among the Western powers; the predominance of finance capital; and the unequal geopolitical development of capitalism[11] demonstrate nothing more than that capitalism had entered into a period of convulsions and more likely of gradual change at the end of the nineteenth and the beginning of the twentieth century. He did not demonstrate that monopoly capitalism is really "moribund" or the "last stage" of capitalism.

Subsequent historical events demonstrated that neither Lenin's theoretical objectives nor his recommended methodology was conducive to creating a socialist society based on proletarian elements. Perhaps the fault lay also in the way in which Lenin envisioned the first steps in the socialization process. He saw socialization as starting with the act of nationalization. But these two concepts share few common characteristics. In the Marxist interpretation, nationalization is an official act of a class that is mastering political power and that forcefully transfers material goods, mainly productive goods (owned by the bourgeoisie or anybody else for that matter) from personal to state ownership. Marxist ideology recognizes the state as a coercive instrument in the hands of a group or class (the bourgeoisie under capitalism, the proletariat under socialism) in order to impose its interests and will on the other groups and classes and, if necessary, to suppress their opposition; ergo, the state cannot be considered as an institution set up through the consent and for the benefit of the whole society. Therefore the transfer of property from private to state ownership does not necessarily mean that the given property will become public. The Bolsheviks have never been able to overcome the ambiguity existing between state and public property.

This characteristic of partiality on the part of the state apparatus can be found both in the Western democracies and in proletarian states. There may be differences in degrees of partiality depending on the degree of democratic development and the amount of mass activism in a particular society, but nevertheless a given amount of partiality always exists. Except for some state functions such as public health, environmental protection, public security, etc., the state's partiality can be observed in almost all its manifestations, although private interests influence these activities, too. Basically this is normal. As long as there are divergent interests in the society and these interests are advanced mainly through the coercive power of the state, the interests of one group or another will prevail in different periods of history.

Throughout all his works, Lenin recognized the partiality of the proletarian state, but as in the case of communist party structure, where he envisioned the interests of the revolutionary avant garde as identical with the interests of the whole proletariat, here, also, the interests of the proletariat are presented as the interests of all the working classes. Postrevolutionary events, though, proved that although these interests coincided in some aspects at that time, they diverged in later historical developments. Judging the issue from this point of view the Leninist nationalization of productive goods cannot be considered a transformation of private property into public property. In times when only labor is shared in common and productive goods are only partially shared we cannot really talk about a "socialization" process. What may have happened in this historical period is that the system of ownership suffered partial modifications in the sense that property was no longer privately held but transformed into collective property to a limited extent. In other words those social groups that controlled the state also exercised some ownership prerogatives, as reflected in the control over the means of production. The whole equation was simplified to "whoever owns the state controls the goods." Therefore what at that time was believed to be an act of "socialization," in fact, was a continuation of a monopoly capitalist framework with partially modified ownership relations.

CHAPTER III

The Leninist Concept of the "Dictatorship of the Proletariat"

Another crucial element of the Leninist theory concerns the idea of the "dictatorship of the proletariat." This idea is closely intertwined with the concept of the state and with the state's role as an administrator of the proletarian dictatorship.

Marx wrote relatively little about the dictatorship of the proletariat yet the idea recurred in Marxist literature with increasing frequency. In its matured form the "dictatorship of the proletariat" was presented as a transitory device to secure temporary leadership and supervisory powers for the industrial proletariat over the entire society in order to enable this class to fulfill its historical role in eradicating exploitation and democratizing the social, political, and economic life.

In the early period of Leninism this idea was interpreted only as an instrument to supplement the abating revolutionary zest of a bourgeoisie already grown old and conservative and to secure the continuity of a predicted new wave of democratic revolutions. In his work "Two Tactics of Social-Democracy in the Democratic Revolution," Lenin wrote:

> Without doubt, Marx and Engels were historically and politically right in thinking that the primary interest of the working class was to drive the bourgeois revolution as far as possible.[1]

Later, the meaning of "proletarian dictatorship" was widened to the proportions of a politico-economic system and its duration extended to cover a whole historical period. During this period the proletariat was expected to gradually obtain political supremacy and to eliminate the last resistance of the bourgeoisie.

The overriding importance which this theory gained in Leninist thought was due, among other things, to the empirical problems of "socialist construction" which the Bolsheviks faced after the insurrectionary period ended. Lenin conceived the dictatorship of the proletariat, not only as a catalyst in the bourgeois-democratic revolution and a leading force in the socialist revolution, but also as a practical tool for social and economic reorganization in a post-insurrectionary era.

The various reevaluations and additions which subsequently affected the theory of "proletarian dictatorship" reveal both the objective development of a theory which must undergo changes under the pressures of historical reality, and also the political expediency so profusely demonstrated by Bolshevik practice. It must be remembered though that a limited political and revolutionary role is reserved for the proletariat also in other early Leninist considerations about the bourgeois-democratic revolution:

> It is the march of events that will, in the democratic revolution, inevitably impose upon us such a host of allies from among the petty bourgeoisie and the peasantry, whose real needs will demand the implementation of our minimal programme that *any concern over a transition to the maximum programme is simply absurd.* (emphasis supplied)[2]

Therefore around 1905 Lenin was still expecting that the conditions for a bourgeois-democratic revolution would last for a long period and sharing political power with other social forces, besides the proletariat, was accepted as a historical necessity. At this time Lenin reserved for the proletariat the role of catalyst in securing the "right" direction in the process of social development. Socialist aims were still considered more an academic issue than something to deal with immediately and concretely. Bourgeois democracy was still considered the major environment in which to prepare the terrain for a political takeover by the proletariat. A transitional period (dictatorship of the proletariat) was seen as necessary while quantitative growth of proletarian consciousness took place and political clout was effectuated amid a capitalist type of economy. However, the extent and the time frame of such a period was never fully clarified. After the October Revolution, when the Bolsheviks faced a weak opposition from different bourgeois and socialist parties, the temptation for power overcame reason and the essence of the dictatorship of the proletariat was revised in the sense that the exercise of political power was restricted only to the proletariat, democracy was rejected as a "superfluous bourgeois institution" and the "withering away of the state" was postponed for an undetermined future. The theory of the "dictatorship of the proletariat" now appears in a persistent way, and is purposeful and detailed while socialism is still covered with a *nebulae* of mystical predictions. Political aims and relations between the proletariat and other social classes and strata are minutely defined in order to achieve what the Bolsheviks called the socialist targets of the revolution. Political policy is now supplemented with an economic program of capitalist expropriation and a differentiated social policy toward the complex spectrum of a stratified social reality. In this program the peasantry was singled out as the last representative of the capitalist system.

In October 1919 Lenin wrote:

> The economic system of Russia in the era of the dictatorship of the proletariat, represents the struggle of labour, united on communist principles on the scale of a vast state and making its first steps–the struggle against petty commodity production and against the capitalism which still persists and against that which is newly arising on the basis of petty commodity production.[3]

In another book Lenin describes the proletariat as exercising its dictatorship in order to deprive the bourgeoisie of its political and economic power, to "neutralize" the peasant class in general and to impose a selective policy on different peasant strata in particular.[4] Perhaps it was the peasant issue in which, in its empirical forms, the "dictatorship of the proletariat" presented the sharpest internal contradictions in content and the greatest bent toward political opportunism. First, the Leninist theory of the "dictatorship of the proletariat" looks upon the whose mass of peasantry as natural allies of the proletariat in the struggle for social democratization (bourgeois-democratic revolution). Later, in a more advanced stage, that of "socialist revolution," the peasantry is looked upon as a heterogeneous class with divided economic interests, therefore with a differentiated political taste. The selective treatment of the peasantry is presented as a matter of historical logic. This policy is varied in the different stages of the socialist revolution, from the "political neutralization" of the whole peasantry, in the early stages, to the outright annihilation of the wealthy peasant strata (Kulaks), and the concomitant neutralization of the middle strata, and an "alliance" with the poor strata in the subsequent stages of the revolution. At this stage the Leninists expected that the victory of socialism in agriculture (collectivism) would reach parity with the socialism previously reached in industry.

According to this plan the first step taken by the Bolsheviks after the successful coup in October was publishing and implementing the "Decree Relating to Land,"[5] which by and large satisfied the century-old land hunger of the peasant by expropriating the big estates. It was a clever move to secure peasant support for the Bolsheviks bid for political power. But it was not a sincere move. The Bolsheviks knew that the creation of a considerable number of small properties would work against their goal of massive expropriation, centralization, and control over production which they perceived as the culmination of the socialist revolution. The peasants did not have to wait for the disappointments of collectivization to change their views on the workings of the "proletarian dictatorship." The rigors of the civil war and the coercive food requisitions soon alienated the whole peasantry. Facing economic disaster and political isolation the Bolsheviks were forced to retreat to the neutral grounds of the proto-capitalist economy of NEP. This retreat was recognized by Lenin himself when he wrote:

> The dictatorship of the proletariat displeased the peasants especially where there was abundance of bread, for the Bolsheviks insisted with great firmness that excess of cereals must be sold to the state at fixed, legal prices, consequently, the peasant classes of the Urals, of Siberia, and the Ukraine sided with Koltchak and Denikin.[6]

The collectivization of agriculture, during the Stalinist era, achieved by intimidation, mass deportation, and brutality, touched even the poor strata of the peasantry. Their reaction clearly demonstrated that any steps toward socialization of agriculture would be met with hostility, therefore accepted only through coercive implementation. More than once history has demonstrated that the immediate and expressed interests of the peasantry lie in the private ownership of the land.

When Stalin forced collectivization upon the Soviet peasants, he inadvertently placed the Bolsheviks in the same dock of the juridical court of history where Lenin tried to place the bourgeoisie when he quoted Marx as saying:

> The French bourgeoisie of 1789 stood firmly on the side of its peasant ally when the German bourgeoisie of 1848 betrayed them without the least compunction.[7]

Again the irony of history came to the fore; socialism whether "utopian" or "scientific," was intended by its founders to fulfill the social will and to solve the producers' alienation, from the beginning was resisted, or at the best hesitantly accepted, by the very people for whose benefit it was created. Peasant policy was not the only issue to be given a new meaning. The principle of democracy was also reevaluated when in March 1919, at the first Congress of the Communist International Lenin said:

> The old, i.e., bourgeois democracy and the parliamentary system, were so organized that it was the mass of working people who were kept

farthest away from the machinery of government. Soviet power, i.e., the dictatorship of the proletariat, on the other hand, is so organized as to bring the working people close to the machinery of government.[8]

He was only two years away from the Kronstadt rebellion against Bolshevik political rule. The social composition of the "rebels," peasants and workers, clearly proved that the laboring classes already felt alienated from the existing political power structure.

In his pamphlet "The Dictatorship of the Proletariat and Elections to the Constituent Assembly," Lenin abandons the concepts of democracy and reaches for alternatives:

> Universal suffrage furnishes a means of measuring the extent to which the classes comprehend their duties. It shows how they tend to resolve the questions presented to them. *Decisions, however, are not made by the vote but by every form of the class struggle up to, and including Civil War.*[9] (emphasis supplied)

Therefore, the decision-making process, one of the signs of political power, is not decided by vote–in other words by the masses–but by some obscure circumstance of "a class struggle." If the success of the class struggle, according to the same Leninist logic, depends on the preparedness, professionalism, and determination of a "revolutionary elite" personified by the Communist Party, the implied necessity to restrict the political monopoly to that small circle of revolutionaries becomes obvious. Lenin never fully explained how the proletariat could exercise its political leadership prior, during, and after the establishment of the proletarian dictatorship, if its political power was circumscribed by its very own party.

The shift from the principle of socialist democracy to the concept of supreme party leadership and from there to the practice of party political monopoly was made relatively quickly during Lenin's administration of the party and the Soviet state. After his death this process continued at an accelerated pace. What caused Lenin to put more emphasis on the dictatorship of the proletariat as the instrument of change rather than choosing the more familiar system of bourgeois-type democracy?

Would not the alternative approach, postponement of the political takeover by the laboring classes for a few decades have been safer and less traumatic?

Lenin rejected such an argument because all his theories were built precisely on the theoretical assumption that socialism was imminent and the proletariat was ripe and ready, if not immediately then in the near future, for the role of hegemon in a socialist revolution and the consequent implementation of socialism. In a close analysis it comes to light that the immanency of socialism was mostly argued by Lenin on the basis of particularities offered by Russia, especially by a defeated Russia: economic and political chaos, all political parties in disarray, a weak and inexperienced middle class. In other words his argument was based more on the weakness of his opponents and less on the strength and preparedness of his alleged hegemon class.

To be sure, Lenin's choice of proletarian dictatorship was not a master plan for securing the class domination of the party elite that was allegedly developed well before the October Revolution. The fervent idealism of the majority of the old Bolshevik guard is witness against such a hypothesis. Neither does the disorganized political status of the bourgeois, peasant, and labor parties solely explain why the Bolsheviks chose the alternative of political monopoly.

It may be that after power fell into their hands, the Bolsheviks realized the utter unpreparedness of the masses for practical leadership, as the initial Marxist theory had expected from the proletariat. The cultural backwardness, the semiliteracy and lack of managerial skills displayed by the industrial working class placed the feasibility of hegemony of this class beyond the realm of political reality.

The frequently recurring talk about the "dictatorship of the proletariat," the postponement of the theory of "withering away of the state," and the fear of "bourgeois ideological influences" on the proletariat point to this conclusion.

If we accept this hypothesis, then Lenin may have been compelled to choose between, as he perceived it, two negative alternatives, both giving the proletariat a respite to prepare itself for hegemony; either the industrial workers would share political power with other social classes, which would have automatically postponed the "socialization" of the means of production (this alternative in Leninist thought was considered tantamount to a slow return to capitalism), or the slogan of the "dictatorship of the proletariat" would be introduced without the direct participation of the proletariat. Actually, it was behind such an empty slogan that the dictatorship of the party elite was evolving.

The rift between what Lenin expected and what the reality offered is depicted in Lenin's changing assessment of the modalities in which the socialist revolution could be achieved.

In 1905 he wrote:

> ...the issue of power (even if partial, episodic, etc.) obviously presupposes participation not only of social-democrats, and not only of the proletariat. This follows from the fact that it is not the proletariat alone that is interested and takes an active part in a democratic revolution. It follows from the insurrection being a 'popular' one, ...with nonproletarian groups, i.e., the bourgeoisie, also taking part in it.[10]

In 1919, however, he reassessed his theory:

> It would be sheer nonsense to think that the most profound revolution in human history, the first case in the world of power being transformed from the exploiting minority to the exploited majority, could take place within the time-worn framework of the old, bourgeois, parliamentary democracy, without drastic changes, without the creation of new forms of democracy, new institutions that embody the new conditions for applying democracy, etc.[11]

The "new forms of democracy" proved to be nothing else but the dictatorship of the proletariat. Between these two statements only fourteen years elapsed. Accepting the Marxist hypothesis that political manifestations are reflections of "objective" necessities created by economic and social needs, then the political manifestation of a bourgeois democracy should reflect the needs of an economic setup imposed by the "independent" and "objective" development of the means of production. Anything qualitatively less or more in the political superstructure could not fit the "objective" requirements of that particular economic setup. The actual examples in political history prove that economic development takes a long period of time before its effects induce any substantial change in the political superstructure. Lenin has never explained how the Russian economy of 1919, actually destroyed and bankrupt, miraculously evolved so impetuously and abruptly that a sudden change was necessary from bougeois-democracy, on which Russia embarked in February 1917, to proletarian dictatorship in October 1917. Seven months of economic stagnation could not warrant such a change in policy. Was it not rather the fear that in an open political competition even the less developed Russian bourgeoisie would hold the field against the inexperienced proletariat?

It is no coincidence that in 1920 Lenin wrote:

> [The communist] must soberly follow the actual state of the class-consciousness and preparedness of the entire class (not only of its communist vanguard), and all the working people (not only of their advanced elements).[12]

It may seem that this fear, coming from the realization of proletarian impotence in complex politics, induced Lenin to postpone the "leadership" of the "leaders" and to entrust it to the revolutionary intelligentsia of the party. Although Lenin never elucidates the supposed duality of power existing between the proletariat and the Bolshevik Party, the reality may suggest that such a duality never actually existed. Surely this Leninist solution of the question of hegemony was originally intended to be only temporary but its transiency, in time, became permanent. History did not fulfill Lenin's expectations: the political maturation of the proletariat was too slow a process to inspire any hope for a future demonstration of proletarian initiative and the moral fiber of the party elite was too weak to resist the temptation of power. In time it became more and more obvious that the dictatorship of the proletariat, originally meant as a temporary device to monitor and influence the bourgeois-democratic revolution and later to suppress the last vestiges of bourgeois resistance, was developing features of permanency. More than that: the proletarian dictatorship let its oppressive hand be felt not only by the "class enemies" of the revolution, but also by the very working class which was supposed to exercise it.

Where did Marxism-Leninism fail in its theory of proletarian hegemony? Is it not a simplified and limited approach to the entire process of historical change inspired by the Marxist-Leninist doctrine that economic inequality results in social and political inequality, a situation which creates the conditions for the existence of class struggle? This class struggle then becomes the main force in social change. While it is true that class struggle, in its varied forms, expresses the seething problems which beset a society in its development, the mere existence of this struggle does not prove that it is always aimed at achieving radical change and not at minor modifications, as is the situation in most historical cases. History has proved that it is not the class struggle that is essential for qualitative social changes, but the existence of a social class, which in its complex composition is capable of creating a new economic system and of applying new forms of technology, science and culture. Under these conditions "class struggle" is reduced to the minor role of a vehicle to achieve the goals of the new class. The existence of a class struggle, even in a violent form, is not yet a sign that the society is on the verge of a serious change. Therefore, class profile, creativeness, spirit of innovation and leadership are what count in the process of change. Does the proletariat possess a revolutionary spirit? Perhaps. But revolutionary spirit can be, in some instances, more destructive than creative. Was the proletariat actually destined to be the harbinger of socialism? There is no socio-political argument to substantiate such a statement. Abstracting class peculiarities, we always find, in different stages of the history of civilization, two distinctive groups: initiators and

executors. Never in history, though, have the initiators or executors perpetuated their class stereotypes into other historical
periods or assumed the same social role which distinguished
them in the previous period. Neither did they ever change their
social function as long as they were fused into an integral class.
Nobody can sustain the notion that the ancient Roman aristocracy became *in corpore* the new feudal aristocracy or that the
slaves of ancient times became automatically feudal serfs. Neither did the feudal aristocracy undergo a metamorphosis into the
capitalists of the modern age or the feudal serfs become transformed into the industrial working class. Historical experience
demonstrates that instead a new social class is the gathering
place for all those individuals who embody the characteristics
and requirements which will constitute the fundamental features
of that class in formation. All those individuals may trace their
origin back to the entire social spectrum of the previous society
and not only from a single group. What made Lenin think that the
proletariat was an exception? The relationship between initiators
and executors is a complex one and increases in complexity
proportionately with the development of technology and culture.
There is a different relationship between initiators and executors
in ancient, medieval, and modern times when the initiators
enforced their directives upon the executors both by socio-
political and economic means. The impact of either method
differed from one age to another. In ancient and medieval periods
extra-economic means prevailed while in modern times economic methods of coercion have proved to be more successful,
though a return to the previous method is obviously demonstrated by the rise of modern totalitarianism. What methods were
to prevail in the proletarian dictatorship and for how long? The
obvious fact that the proletariat carried out its role as executor in
the capitalist system and was unable to assume a new role as
social leader, came to be realized slowly by the Bolsheviks and
is not yet fully understood. Caught up in their revolutionary
momentum the Bolsheviks underestimated the historical fact
that the proletariat cannot fulfill its "historical role" as social
equalizer, consequently, prompted by the misery of the masses

and the bondage of their own philosophy, which demanded social equality, they embarked upon a process of destroying the existing entrepreneurial elements without replacing them with other creative social forces. The dilemma they created was to be solved by transforming the hollow dictatorship of the proletariat slogan into a factual dictatorship of the revolutionary intelligentsia and to extend this dictatorship into an undetermined future.

It seems possible that the collision between Lenin's theoretical juggling and historical reality was due, among other things, to his overestimation of the social effects of the economic expropriation which he and his party considered a priority of their revolutionary program. Lenin may have assumed that the expropriation effectuated during the period of the "dictatorship of the proletariat" would automatically place the society on a track toward socialism and would solve all economic, social, psychological, and cultural problems which the society inherited from capitalism. Expropriation was equated with socialization. Basically, expropriation is a deliberate political act which changes the ownership of either a limited segment, or most, of the society's productive goods. This change can have the partial effects of the expropriations effectuated after World War II in England or France, or the radical effects of those executed in Eastern Europe and previously in the Soviet Union. Land reform, for example, is such a process in which one form of private property (big estates) is transformed into another form of private property (small land holdings). In this case the institution of private ownership is not altered.

Private property can also be transformed into collective property, for example, when private lands and industries are transferred into state property or cooperative property.

Here I would like to emphasize that even collective property, cannot always be considered public property, which would imply ownership prerogatives for the whole nation and not only for a small collective of cooperators or a group of political leaders holding state power. Transferring productive goods into state property actually does not achieve the socialization of these goods unless the society is able to find institutional ways to control the state apparatus and thereby use the state to implement its ownership prerogatives, such as: the right to institute or terminate productive units or to rent or sell them, and direct access to the managerial decision-making process. Expropriation has a more limited economic and social impact than socialization because it does not have the penetrative and lasting effect of the latter. Many social, cultural, and psychological facets of the human existence are only partially affected by the expropriation process and in most cases they remain unchanged. Even in a case where private ownership is transformed into collective ownership, the degree of collectivization may differ widely. In communist societies during recent times, though, neither state nor cooperative property ever reached the stage of being fully public property as required by any socialist ideology. The problem with expropriation is that it places the accent on the destruction of one form of ownership without having the certainty that the alternative solution will be superior or at least have the same potentialities as the previous form of ownership. Historical experience amply demonstrates that most of the expropriations effectuated were motivated less by a regard for a higher productivity and more by considerations of social justice.

Socialization, on the other hand, cannot be the result of an *ad hoc* and conscious political act. It can come about only when technological and human development bring the individual to such a degree of consciousness that his individual and social interests coincide in a common set of principles. These two categories, logically, are two faces of the same coin. They relate and condition each other. Today we cannot envisage extensive human development (knowledge, culture, sophistication) without an adequate degree of technological development, nor a highly advanced technology without highly cultured individuals. In other words, socialism may be achieved not through a simple act of expropriation, but as a result of the inner growth, on a social level, of the individual who can and is willing to accept the idea of total collectivism. Such a level may be achieved, again theoretically, when technology, through automation, can create such an abundance of material goods that the produced goods will not represent any exchange value and therefore will not be the object of competition, and the production of these goods will be achieved without the use of any economic or extra-economic coercive measures.

The Bolsheviks missed the point when they emphasized only the quantitative and concentrated development of productive forces (heavy industry) and gave less emphasis to the development of technology and even less to the development of those productive facilities which directly satisfy the human needs and which would have created an ambiance for human development. Mass and concentrated production is not a "socialist" invention, it is already obtained in the capitalist system through the huge trusts and multinational corporations, which in any case, have achieved much better results as far as productivity and a balanced economy is concerned. As many authors have already pointed out, the obsession of the Bolsheviks with industrial progress resulted in the neglect of the human factor. In the Bolshevik program the human being's role is only to join in mechanical fusion to the machine as a manipulator of the productive process. The worker's interests, his theoretical potentiality as innovator or manager, and his willingness to embark on a process which hypothetically would lead to full collectivism, were utterly neglected or hidden behind empty slogans.

While one can predict the main lines and direction of technological development, the evolution of a superior human behavior is still in the domain of speculative thinking. Up to this time no socialist society has been able to present any traces of those qualities which might characterize the "new" and "socialist" man.

If one removes the ideological idealizations from empirical socialism, the only remaining reality would be the element of uniformity, aimed at reaching the maximum potential of quantitative economic development. Again, this is another area in which capitalism has been far more successful than any of the so-called "socialist" societies which have come into existence up to this time.

Only when capitalism reaches a level of development which can integrate and standardize not only the production of consumer goods but also the people's psychological and cultural characteristics—only then will humanity perhaps be ready for socialism. Practical experience has proved that any shortcuts proposed by the revolutionary elite, by means of expropriation, were compelled to return to a form of modified capitalism. In carrying out the expropriation of the Russian bourgeoisie the Bolsheviks found themselves confronting the dilemma of previous revolutions in which enthusiasm and idealism, mixed with a good dose of naiveté, brought the revolutionary movement well beyond the necessary limits of solving the problems which caused the revolution in the first place. Once the expropriation was done, the Bolsheviks realized that the proletariat failed to step in and "fulfill its historical mission." The proletariat remained the executors, as they were during capitalism. The Bolsheviks succeeded in expropriation but failed in socialization.

This was to have serious consequences for the attempt to establish a socialist society, more exactly a socialist society with a proletarian hegemony. It resulted in a radical and permanent separation of the revolutionaries from the laborers, preserving the same dichotomous setup inherited from the prerevolutionary era.

It was during the Stalinist period that Marxist-Leninist expectations of socialism were confronted by the stern reality of the impossibility of achieving it, at least not in the present historical period. The void left by the disintegration of the socialist dream was soon filled by those careerist elements eager to carve out a position in the new economic organization where their common interests and preoccupations, as organizers of production, forged them into a new entrepreneurial class.

It cannot be said that the changes in official policy of the Communist Party and its effects on class relations were totally different from the reality which Lenin bequeathed to Stalin. There remained the same dichotomous social setup which the revolution tried but was unable to abolish. The only major change, that in the upper levels of the society, was already achieved with the accession to power by the Bolsheviks in

October 1917, and only perfected by the Stalinists. The political leadership refused to hand the power over to the proletariat, and the proletariat would have been unable to receive it even if it had been offered. The permanency of this situation was a fact which became more and more obvious in the Stalinist era.

The appearance of a separate class of revolutionary leaders whose barely consolidated leadership position was soon challenged by other leading groups involved in economic management demonstrates that the process of social and economic transformation was far from being concluded. A barely detected movement of economic managers whose economic methodology remained inside the capitalist framework slowly prevailed under the new conditions of state ownership.

CHAPTER IV

"SOCIALIST" PERSPECTIVES UNDER STALIN

For those who study the Stalin era it is obvious that the essential changes which occurred during that period were not so much in the social and political structure, where despite some tangible changes, the actual disparity between the toiling masses and a privileged leadership, inherited from the previous regime, continued and in time even grew. The significant changes appeared more in those theoretical egalitarian principles inherited from Marxist ideology which were intended to guide Soviet society toward the realization of a communist society. The profoundness of these empirical and theoretical changes is demonstrated by the permanence of the essential social, economic and political forms and organizations which were shaped in this particular period and which still persisted after the main performer, Stalin, disappeared from the scene.

But how deep did these changes run? Some Soviet analysts compare the Stalin period, especially during the later 1920s, with the revolution of 1917, even calling this so-called third revolution greater as far as structural changes are concerned. There is much dissension on this subject among the scholars, who disagree about the size and intensity of these changes; their quantitative and qualitative impact on the future development of "socialism;" the depth of the ideological metamorphosis; the volume of Marxist and Leninist ideas exhibited in Stalinism; whether Stalinism was a direct continuation of Leninism or just those reemphasized Leninist ideas which were paving the way for the totalitarian system; and, whether Stalinism was a betrayal of Marxist principles as the leaders of the opposition claimed.

The vastness of the subject exceeds the size of this essay which compels the author to analyze only those facets which directly concern the main aspects of Marxist ideology. There can be no doubt that Stalinism is permeated with Marxism and Leninism, that there is a continuity of principles from Marxism to Leninism and from Leninism to Stalinism. What is determinant, though, in the Stalinist equation, is that some facets of the ideology were overemphasized in order to achieve some practical political goals, and others were altogether dropped due to their incompatibility with empirical reality. Although the problem of the incompatibility of some Marxist ideas with historical facts was already apparent in the works of Marx, especially in those sections concerning the building of socialism, the burden of solving these contradictions had to be borne by Lenin, who endeavored to apply Marxist tenets to an economically backward peasant society totally unlike that envisioned by Marx. This situation compelled Lenin to make considerable alterations in Marxist theory, especially concerning the premises of the socialist revolution and the methodology of socialist construction. As Daniels pointed out:

> Without acknowledging the fact, and probably without even realizing it, Lenin introduced (or at least set in motion) momentous changes in the substance of Marxian belief.[1]

In this perspective it can be said that Stalin's job was somewhat easier. In his lesser intellectualism Stalin didn't bother himself with refined ideas, paradoxes, or even outright contradictions. Fitted with a practical personality, politics, goals, and achievements played a greater role in his system of priorities. Those ideas which no longer fit reality simply were dropped or branded as a product of bourgeois or petty-bourgeois ideology.

But the difficulties in applying Marxist precepts extended beyond Russia into Western Europe. The way in which the Western proletariat acted was another puzzling problem crying for the revision of Marxism. The problem that "the masses if left to themselves, would not become revolutionary"[2] posed the strong probability of the proletariat's inability to initiate and implement an autonomous political strategy. This was not a new revelation to Marx and Engels, especially after their experience with the Paris Commune, but later the problem became more acute, especially in the historical period when Lenin was politically active. This may explain the strong paternalistic tone toward the proletariat, evident in Lenin's works and continued at an enhanced level under Stalin. This was not only due to the autocratic propensities of the dictator, but was also a response to the specific social requirements imposed by the immediate necessity of implementing a quasi-new economic system. This system had already found its rationalization in Lenin's works.

Interpretations of Stalin vary. They range from the image created by the regime itself to the negative image depicted by its opponents and include more balanced analyses by some Western scholars. To be sure, Stalin's and the Stalinists' position was that their actions developed directly from Marxist-Leninist ideas, and that none of them, including their voluntarist actions, vitiated the spirit of Leninism. They considered their activity to be the only possible way to solve the multiple problems besetting their country at that particular time. They believed that their actions were "a determined offensive against the capitalist elements in town and country."[3] They simplified the issue to the point that for all practical purposes there were only two ways open to action: the "capitalist way," which would have hindered the building of socialism by a lack of an active, militant policy, especially toward agriculture, and would have negative repercussions as well for the industrial sector; or the "socialist way," which would have upset the delicate balance between the peasantry and the proletariat in the favor of the latter.

Their opponents' views were just the opposite. They considered Stalinism to be a blatant deviation from the Marxist line and an outright betrayal of the socialist revolution. Trotsky's theory of Stalinism as a "bonapartist" perversion is illuminating in itself. This leading personality of the Bolshevik Revolution points to

the sliding of Stalinism away from Marxism and toward totalitarianism but describes this phenomenon as a temporary necessity resulting from the economic backwardness which hindered
any immediate possibility of achieving equality.

> If the state does not die away [writes Trotsky] but grows more and more
> despotic, if the plenipotentiaries of the working class become bureau-
> cratized, and the bureaucracy rises above the new society, this is not for
> some secondary reasons like the psychological relics of the past, etc.,
> but as a result of the iron necessity to give birth to and support a
> privileged minority so long as it is impossible to guarantee genuine
> equality.[4]

This leads Trotsky to reject the official Soviet statement: "We
have not yet, of course, complete communism, but we have
already achieved socialism—that is, the lowest stage of communism."[5] Trotsky's argument points out that the official Soviet
explanation does not exhaust the whole range of the Marxian
approach. The existence of state and cooperative property—which
Trotsky considers socialist property—was not yet the sign that the
lower stage of communism was achieved. Only "a society which
from the beginning stands higher in its economic development
than the most advanced capitalism"[6] can be considered a communist society of lower stage. As such, Trotsky considered the
Soviet Union under Stalin "not a socialist regime, but a prepara-
tory regime transitional from capitalism to socialism..."[7] and the
official Soviet statement as a deviationist interpretation of
Marxism. Trotsky considers the Soviet experiment to be a
revolutionary process which in its incipient form started as a
socialist movement but due to the economic backwardness of the
country, the bureaucratization of the party, and the extravagance
of its leaders, it departed from egalitarian socialist ideas and
temporarily took the form of a bourgeois state. "For the defense
of 'bourgeois law' the workers' state was compelled to create a
'bourgeois' type of instrument—that is, the same old gendarme,
although in a new uniform."[8] Aside from considering the bourgeois features of the Soviet state as temporary phenomena,

Trotsky fails to explain why the newly created bureaucracy really needed a "super arbiter," or "emperor," which could only result in a cult of personality. Trotsky also failed to demonstrate convincingly that the parallel between Soviet bonapartism and fascism was the result of the belatedness of the world revolution.[9] That Stalinism actually was part of a profound process of social transformation, with obvious features of permanency, in no way implies that this transformation was socialist in nature. This process which started with the Bolshevik revolution and developed via Stalinism, continued to evolve until the present day, preserving many institutions and ideas that appeared during Stalin's era.

A representative of Western scholarship, Herbert Marcuse, believes that in both ideological and empirical politics the break between Leninism and Stalinism was serious. He writes:

> The differences between the first years of the Bolshevik Revolution and the fully developed Stalinist state are obvious; they readily appear as the steady growth of totalitarianism and authoritarian centralization, as the growth of the dictatorship not of but over the proletariat and peasantry.[10]

Yet he also recognizes the continuation of Leninist elements by affirming the applicability of the dialectical law of transformation of (Leninist) quantity (that is, Lenin's theories) into (Stalinist) quality (Stalinist empiricism). Unlike many other interpreters of Soviet ideology, Marcuse believes that Soviet ideology, especially that related to the Stalin period, is more than a rationalization of official policies, but that its development reflected the actual realities of Soviet life,[11] and its evolution was influenced by the impact of the "interaction between Soviet and Western society."[12] From which it may be concluded that the forces which shape Soviet policy are determined not only by internal pressures and necessities but in equal, if not greater measure, by the political and economic actions of the Western world.

Concerning the socialist content of Stalinist ideology, Marcuse is rather skeptical. He thinks that it cannot be considered socialist ideology "in the sense envisaged by Marx and Engels,"[13] since it cannot reflect socialist reality. To Marcuse, Stalinism is rather the spirit of a necessity to industrialize, although he assumes that the initial goals of the Bolsheviks were socialist. For Marcuse it is irrelevant whether the Soviet leadership is really guided by Marxist principles or not:

> ...once incorporated into foundational institutions and objectives of the new society, Marxism becomes subject to a historical dynamic which surpasses the intentions of the leadership and to which the manipulators themselves succumb.[14]

This belief in the objectivity of the historical process is obvious. But it is a historical process which reflects the need for industrialization and for closing the economic gap with the West, rather than the need for socialism.

As for the character of Soviet ideology, Marcuse writes:

> Soviet Marxism has assumed the character of a 'behavioral science.' Most of its theoretical pronouncements have a pragmatic, instrumentalist intent; they serve to explain, justify, promote, and direct certain actions and attitudes which are actual 'data' for these pronouncements. These actions and attitudes are rationalized and justified in terms of the inherited body of 'Marxism-Leninism' which the Soviet leadership applies to the changing historical situation.[15]

The frequent changes in policy reflected in parallel changes in ideology are less expressions of the instability of Soviet politics and more the reflections of those issues of pressing urgency related to the emergence and evolution of Soviet society. These issues forced upon Lenin a need to make correctional changes, a need which during the Stalin period became even more acute. The failure of both Western and Soviet proletariat to act as an independent revolutionary class compelled Soviet ideologists to look for ideological alternatives which in due time were to be translated into empirical action and served as a political guide for the Soviet state.

As I have already mentioned, some of the changes were not necessarily new to Marxist ideology. At times the overemphasis on some Marxist principles sufficed to justify some political actions which otherwise would have contradicted Marxist ideology as a whole. For instance, Marx distinguished between two "phases" in socialist construction. The first phase, dedicated to the development of the productive forces and the productivity of labor, becomes overemphasized in Soviet ideology to the detriment of socialist goals, which are delayed indefinitely. The repressive social and political policy arising from the necessity for economic regimentation are officially presented as self-imposed by the proletariat through its own state, and the lack of any theoretical or empirical limits on the intensity and duration of this repression inadvertently transforms, for all practical purposes, the means of "socialist" construction into an end in itself.

Another Marxist ideological statement given an added emphasis was the distinction between real (historic) and immediate (economic) interests of the proletariat. Because of the failure of the proletariat to realize "its historical mission" and to act in a revolutionary manner, when even the Russian proletariat rose up only within a bourgeois democratic framework during the February Revolution, a rupture between the proletariat and the Bolshevik leaders became inevitable after the October coup. This inability of the proletariat to rise about its immediate economic interests compelled the Communist Party to extend the "dictatorship of the proletariat" over the proletariat itself, explaining this move as identical with the real (historical) interests of the proletariat.

Some characteristic features of Leninism—described by Marcuse—such as "the shift in the revolutionary agent from the class-conscious proletariat to the centralized party as the avant garde of the proletariat and the emphasis on the role of the peasantry as ally of the proletariat,"[16] together with the doctrines of the necessity of a high degree of industrialization and rationalization of the economy and of "socialism in one country," complemented by the theoretical dichotomy between East and West became the cornerstone of Stalinist theory and the basis of Soviet policy.

Notwithstanding these transfers from Leninism, the differences in pragmatic policies between Leninism and Stalinism are numerous and obvious. There were also theories which explained and motivated Stalinist policies while retaining a Leninist essence, but in many instances the ways in which they were implemented were in blatant contradiction with the Leninist spirit, as well as with Marxist statements.

According to Marcuse: "The doctrine of 'socialism' in one country, which provided the general framework for Marxism during the Stalin period, also serves to provide a world-historical justification for the repressive functions of the Soviet state."[17] This increased and repressive role of the state is prescribed by Stalinism as a remedy for the internal contradictions inherent in the Soviet society, and explained as an inheritance of capitalism. Later it served as an indirect catalyst for the lagging international revolutionary movement, evolving in the environment of a politically inactive proletariat and the continuous military strengthening of the capitalist world; even direct intervention in the affairs of the Western world was not excluded. The Stalinist perception of internal contradictions to be solved by the intervention of the centralized state fell in two categories: antagonistic contradictions, predominating over the first stage of socialist construction; and non-antagonistic contradictions that already existed in the first phase but continued into the second stage of socialist implementation. In the first category belongs the contradiction between the socialist state and the bourgeois residues still present in the Soviet society, the contradictions between rich and poor peasants, and the conflicts between the predominantly old consciousness and the rising socialist mentality. In the second category are listed the non-antagonistic contradictions between the proletariat and the "working peasantry" and between mental and physical labor. For Stalin there existed a single and simple answer to all of these social and economic complexities: to reinforce the state machinery, making it omnipotent and omnipresent in all segments of human life. "The highest possible development of the power of the state, decrees Stalin, with the object of preparing the conditions for the dying away of the state—that is the Marxist formula."[18] This concept based on the Leninist idea of continuous existence of the state, with obvious capitalistic features, is officially explained by the fact that the first stage of socialist construction is still "affected" with its capitalist heritage, an idea which in turn is inspired by the original Marxian concept which admits the existence of the state in the first period of socialism. All this juxtaposed by Marcuse with the political reality of the Soviet Union:

> ...the Soviet state exercises throughout political and governmental functions against the proletariat itself; domination remains a specialized function in the division of labor and is as much the monopoly of a political, economic, and military bureaucracy.[19]

The permanency of a situation which retains the obvious characteristics of a class society is explained by Marcuse as the perpetuation of an authoritarian organization, separate from the rest of the population, which is in charge of the productive and distributive mechanisms and is distinct from the "collective control of the ruled population."[20]

Although a general directing function of the state toward society is prescribed by Soviet ideology, actually, the role of the state is furthered to the extreme point when it separates the producers from control over the process of production.[21]

Another feature of the Soviet ideology is the emergence of voluntarism which was especially dominant in the Stalinist period. Everything from simple political issues to complex ideological structures, such as the determination of the superstructure by the economic infrastructure which, according to official opinion acted blindly in capitalism, was now, under "socialist" conditions, the subject of direction and control.

...while the objective, determinist character of dialectical laws is thus strengthened [writes Marcuse] Soviet Marxism in reality appears as defying determinism and practicing voluntarism. The shift in emphasis from the former to the latter seems to be a feature of Leninism and seems to culminate in Stalinism.[22]

The changes and omissions that occurred in the innermost core of Marxist theory were a clear sign that the Soviet regime began to mature. The weakening of the theory of transition from quantity to quality, the denial of the need for changes under socialism, the introduction of the notion of "non-antagonistic contradictions," and the reintroduction of formal logic and the omission of the "negation of the negation"[23] point to a maturing society in need of stability. These changes also indicated that the ruling group was willing to compromise in order to make its members responsible for their actions. Marcuse pointed out that while these changes in themselves did not contradict the basic dialectical concepts of Marxism, "the function of the dialectic itself has undergone a significant change: it has been transformed from a mode of critical thought into a universal 'world outlook' and a universal method with rapidly fixed rules and regulations."[24]

Stalinism's deemphasis of dialectics in history and its subsequent emphasis on the movement of nature can also be explained in the light of the regime's fear of the ultimate conclusion that could be drawn from the dialectical logic, that the dominating regime itself is subject to being surpassed by historical development, and its therefore as frail and replaceable as the regime it just replaced.

These subtle changes had enough impact to transform Marxism from a seemingly objective theoretical outlook into a rigid, institutionalized ideology that was called upon to justify and defend a new system of domination. This crisis in Marxist ideology is observed also by Raymond Bauer as a crisis in which ideological tenets came into more frequent contradiction with the Soviet reality: "...as the history of the Soviet Union unfolded, it became evident that these (Marxist) postulates were untenable in various areas of society...."[25] In this way an ideological crisis developed parallel with the social one and it seems that Stalin realized this dilemma and set himself to resolve it through the legalization and institutionalization of Soviet reality and the adoption of the ideology to that reality. He carried out this aim by solving two important problems: the controversy over the theoretical principles of economic planning and the disagreement between the mechanists and the dialecticians in philosophy.[26] Naturally the outcome was the victory of the teleological approach to economic and social planning and the supremacy of the dialecticians over the mechanists in philosophy.

It would be a mistake to consider Stalin as the conscientious generator of this crisis in order to get rid of dangerous competitors in the process of solving that crisis. The embryos of the crisis were already there and evolved proportionally with the Soviet society. It was not a crisis related to socialism because socialism never surfaced in Russia; it was rather the turmoil of a changing society which was growing into a renovated form a capitalism. Seemingly, Stalin was the unconscious agent whose personal abilities and propensity toward brutality matched the radical requirements of that transitional period. Ironically, the voluntarism so carefully cultivated by Stalinist ideologues as a shortcut toward socialism, serviced only the objective need of a society which was not ready for it.

To blame the predetermined nature of society and its institutions for objective social shortcomings may be helpful during times of upheaval, but when the dust has settled and the new order gears into action on everyday business, it is time to return to the good old voluntarism and its counterpart, individual responsibility. No society, till this time, has been able to survive without these two moral ingredients.

Robert V. Daniels also shares the opinion of those authors who believe that ideologically Stalinism was a deviation from Marxism. He emphasizes the deviationist theory of "socialism in one country" which Stalin propounded in December 1924[27] and the reduction of Marxist-Leninist doctrine to "a mere political device,"[28] changed and applied for the sake of political opportunism, as a means of "...rationalizing action after the fact."[29]

All these inconsistencies between theoretical statements and actual policies, the frequent changes in the policies themselves, and the subsequent strivings to match the theory with the new policies, point to the fact that Bolshevik politics were undergoing a crisis of identity. There was a continuous collision between the objective course of social development and the hypothetical events expected by leaders whose views were permeated by Marxist ideology and who were incapable of judging historical events outside a Marxist framework.

It is certain that the inconsistencies in policy were not the sole product of political cynicism and opportunism. Daniels expresses this conviction when he writes:

> One is tempted to suspect that the party leaders, especially Stalin, were cynically manipulating phrases which they ceased to take seriously, yet the evidence by and large indicates that they were really persuaded of their true orthodoxy, and that the flexibility of policy on which they insisted was enhanced rather than restricted by the aura of orthodoxy which reinterpretation could confer on each new twist and turn.[30]

Further on he also states: "characteristically, these sweeping revisions of Marxist theory came as responses to practical political needs."[31]

In the meantime the economic and social needs translated into political demands for industrialization were advancing with an overwhelming force. The industrialization debate which shook the Soviet society between 1924 and 1928 and the consequent adoption of the first five-year plan for industrialization, with its harsh methods of execution, reflected something more than the immediate economic need to industrialize a backward country for the sake of political and military security. Perhaps this complex issue will become more understandable if placed in a historical perspective.

The process of industrialization which started in Western Europe (England) almost four centuries ago was the result of an economic evolution which reached a point where enough capital, technological knowledge, and skill were accumulated to challenge the old system of production. It was a lonely experiment in which the results and failures of the then new system could be compared only against its previous achievements. Any comparison with the old system was futile due to the radically different structure of the new economic organization. Yet the results of industrialization were tremendous. It changed not only the way in which people produced the necessary goods but it changed their consumption habits, their way of living and thinking, their culture, and ultimately the social intercourse among them. The impact of industrialization spread from England to other parts of Western Europe and North America, and to parts of Asia and Eastern Europe. Although by this time there is hardly a corner of the planet untouched by the fever of industrialization, the intensity of this process varied widely from one country to another. While some were bursting with industrial output and technological innovations, others (and these were the majority) were barely touched by economic modernism and became suppliers of raw materials, reserves of cheap labor, and mostly meager markets for the developed countries. This differentiated development of industry raised the ominous danger of perpetuating the economic and political subordination of the backward to the developed nations.

In his time Trotsky pointed to this situation when he wrote:

> The history of recent decades very clearly shows that, in the conditions of capitalist decline, backward countries are unable to obtain that level which the old centers of capitalism have obtained. Having themselves arrived in a blind alley, the highly civilized nations block the road to those in process of civilization. Russia took the road of proletarian revolution...because she could not develop further on a capitalist basis.[32]

Trotsky's theory is applicable to the point where he implies that the only avenue for further development is the "socialist" way. His theory sees only the necessity of a quantitative growth of industry while actually the main reason for economic restructuring was the new phase into which the technology was ready to enter. In the early and middle phases of capitalist development the historical role of capitalism was to develop a relatively low level of technology which required only small investments of capital obtainable by a limited process of capital accumulation and realized by small entrepreneurs. Later, when technology reached a high and complex level of development, the quantity of capital required to finance such a development became tremendously large and obtainable only by large concentrations of capital. The feeble middle classes of the economically retarded countries had neither the financial resources nor the experience to execute such radial changes involving not only their country's economy but also its cultural and educational profile. The widening economic-technological gap exposed the backward countries to a continuous drain of their resources toward the industrially advanced countries, a drain not matched by a proportional development of their economies. This situation created a permanent social tension and a ground for criticism among those segments of the society (intellectuals, laborers, peasants) negatively influenced by this process. The search for solution, especially for immediate solutions, took many of these societies to the verge of revolution.

The need for structural changes in the capitalist system became obvious. Actually, Marx saw this process of change as taking place by the end of the nineteenth century and confounded it with the necessity to replace capitalism with socialism.

Skipping Trotsky's notion of "capitalist decline" (actually belonging to Marx), and replacing it with the concept of "changing capitalism," we get a more realistic picture of an economic system which cannot fulfill its historical function of changing the world without changing itself. A process of change which involves only some features of capitalism could take place without upsetting the basic dichotomy between the initiators and executors. Economic changes, such as industrialization, concentration of capital, planning, etc., are not necessarily socialist. They could be just developments toward a form of state capitalism achievable either in a "capitalist" or a "socialist" way.

Going back to the abovementioned dichotomous world of developed and underdeveloped nations we can see, as a historical trend, a growing, at times exaggerated suspicion, restlessness, and xenophobia among the newly formed middle classes in the backward nations. By the turn of the century this phenomenon reached an acute stage in Eastern Europe, especially in Russia, and by the post-World War II period in most of the Asian, African and South American countries.

This obsession with the desire to industrialize and to close the gap with the developed countries was inherited by the Bolsheviks, who saw in industrialization not only a means to secure the economic independence and political and military security of the regime but a way to create those economic and social conditions which were for the Marxist ideology a *sine qua non* for the implementation of the socialist idea. But these historical developments still do not cover the truth in all its complexity. There is still the question, among many others, of the form in which industrialization had already taken place in Russia in the pre-revolutionary era and which was by and large adopted by the communist regime after it imposed its rule. This form called for a high degree of centralization and state intervention in the process of industrialization. At a time when industrialization in Western Europe was a product of individual entrepreneurship and keen competition, the latecomers in Eastern Europe had to replace the lack of private initiative with state intervention which, under the conditions of relatively meager private capital and of an inexperienced and small middle class, proved to be the most efficient way to achieve rapid industrialization. As the practical expression of this necessity the Bolsheviks proceeded to an almost immediate nationalization of most industrial means of production. The fact that nationalization for a long period of time proved ineffective and cumbersome from the point of view of efficiency and profitability can be attributed mostly to the lack of technical and financial expertise of the Bolsheviks. During the ensuing civil war they imposed the economic system of war communism, which actually imposed itself upon the regime, due to economic hardship and destruction caused by war. Actually war communism, with all its radical measures, did not fulfill many of the Marxist requirements for a total public ownership and control of the means of production. More socialistic in this period was the distributive process, due to the extraordinary circumstances of a dearth in consumer goods, the immediate necessity to secure the collaboration and support of the proletariat, and, not the least, to give a formal homage to the idealistic communist view still powerful among the Bolsheviks. But even this policy of seemingly socialistic distribution was not entirely democratic. It was the peasantry who had to pay the tab through compulsive surrender of all the meager food supplies which their villages had managed to save.

The NEP period with its partial retreat to capitalist economic methodology was also necessitated by the failure of war communism, which, without achieving the socialistic ideal, provoked the alienation of the peasantry from the Soviet system. NEP, like war communism, proved to be only a temporary remedy promoted by political opportunism. Consequently it may be said that most of the actual socio-economic transformations which fulfilled the historical requirements of the technological explosion, actually started with the Stalin revolution.

Slowly a new meaning was given to socialism—"production socialism," to use Daniels' expression—"where the earlier aims of distributive justice and equality were rudely subordinated to the practical requirements of building, equipping, and operating a modern industrialized economy."[33] But the impact of industrialization went even deeper and the Bolsheviks seemed to realize it. The process of industrialization was more than merely changing from an underdeveloped to a developed status, it meant a process of acculturation which would change not only the ordinary ways of living, but the spiritual and psychological character of the nation. Such a process of transformation was to be channeled and exploited by the new leaders for their own political benefit. In other words what later became more important was not the aim of the process but the methodology used to obtain it.

CHAPTER V

The Illusions Lost

The end of the NEP period signalized the coming of a new interval of change. For some authors, among them Alexander Erlich, the end of NEP was only the result of the fulfillment of the economic goals projected by that economic policy and therefore, "an enlargement of the capacity of growth was necessary."[1]

That the change involved more than a mere quantitative change in industrial development is evidenced by the fiery debates that preceded it between different groups inside the Communist Party. In these debates the fate of the opponents, whether of the right or the left, was sealed by their pervasive idealism, by their inability to adapt to the prosaic interests in material advancement which contained haunting similarities to those of the bourgeoisie which not long ago they had helped to its demise. The depth of these changes was also indicated by those ideological changes, subtle, yet radical in their impact on party policy, that affected the relations between the leaders and laborers in both the urban and rural environment.

Lenin's idealist, radical, and anarchistic attitude in the period immediately prior to the revolution and expressed in his work "State and Revolution" was soon dropped for a return to organizational, business-like activity. He must have realized that revolutionary utopianism was taking his party nowhere. The idea of a "communist state" incorporated into the Bolshevik program in 1917, exhibiting such features as a "democratic-peasant republic," the destruction of the existing state machinery, and the concept of "armed people"[2] were either short-lived or never actually realized. Slowly the idea of a path-breaking, avantgardist minority dictatorship returned to quotidian party life and activity. But this switch to political exclusivism and monopoly, while it proved to be lasting, did not go smoothly. The same opposition groups, of left and right, surfaced and demanded a share in power and policy making. As Daniels pointed out:

> Throughout the early years of the communist regime from 1917 to 1921, this issue of industrial administration had crucial significance for two events. First, it was the most sensitive indicator of the clash of principles about the shaping of the new social order. At the same time, it was the most continuous and provocative focus of actual conflict between communist factions.[3]

The reaction to this political monopolism naturally aroused opposition, not only from inside the Bolshevik Party but from other socialist parties and from the proletariat itself. The socialists outside the Bolshevik organization understandably opposed the undue concentration of power in Bolshevik hands which would exclude them not only from the political arena of decision making but would have denied them any say in the future reorganization of the country as well.

The opposition movement inside the party, though agreeing on some facets of the policy, diverged seriously from the Leninist line on the issue of economic control. The left communists were disappointed with the Leninist relinquishment of their 1917 program of a "stateless society administered spontaneously and democratically by the working class."[4] They still indulged themselves in the illusion of a democratic conclusion of the revolution, expecting control by the masses to exercise itself in all social activities, including economic activity. Like Lenin in his brief intermezzo with utopian expectations, they were apprehensive of a growing state bureaucracy as an alien *corpus* in the *summa* of socialist *dictums*.

More important, though, was the divergence between the proletarian masses and the Bolshevik Party. Attracted by the radical and utopian Bolshevik program of 1917, the workers gathered around the Communist Party and moved, often independently, to establish workers' control over the factories. Factory and plant committees (*fabrichnozavodnye komitety*) mushroomed quickly. These committees, eager to run the industry by themselves, ousted the old management and shortly afterward created a chaotic situation in the economy. The Bolsheviks, not having yet totally secured political control, supported the status quo. Later, though, the Bolsheviks tried to solve the problem of industrial control by backing the trade unions' claim that the central role in organizing the production should belong to them.[5] As Daniels quotes Shliapnikov:

> The trade-union organizations, as class organizations of the proletariat which are constructed according to the industry principle, must take upon themselves the main work of organizing production and restoring the weakened productive forces of the country. Energetic participation in all organs which regulate production, the organization of workers' control...such are the tasks of the day....The trade-union organizations must transform themselves into organs of the socialist state.[6]

The move at that time was actually motivated by the Communist Party's desire to control the proletariat through labor unions that were heavily infiltrated by communist elements. The Bolshevik policy misfired though. It didn't bring about workers' control of industry, which they had to relinquish anyway due to inefficiency, but only shifted the developing antagonism from the workers to the trade unions, which the Bolsheviks later had to deal with.

By 1920 these divergences had reappeared, with the boundaries drawn more clearly. The main divergence was between Leninist theory, brought almost to its Stalinist perfection by Trotsky's plan of militarization of labor, and the workers' interests represented by the trade unions. Though the issue was again the role of the workers in the administration of industry, the battle raged mostly inside the Bolshevik Party, where the ultra-left again expounded their pro-worker, anarcho-utopian socialism.

The Eighth Party Congress, held in March 1919, established the priority of the trade unions in the economy. But that decision was not taken seriously by the Leninists, who used the economic breakdown to justify overall nationalization and centralized governmental administration of the economy. Even if Leninism had relinquished its effort to achieve all-encompassing control of the economy in favor of a takeover by the trade unions, the problem of social polarization as a consequence of a Leninist policy still would not have been solved. Between 1918 and 1919 the trade unions actually played a quasi-autonomous role in industrial administration, with the net result that the more the unions were involved in managerial bureaucracy the "more bureaucratic they became themselves."[7] The only difference would have been that the bureaucratization process, which seems to follow any assumption of power, would have touched the worker element in the union leadership instead of the intellectual element in the party leadership. This alternative was unlikely, however, as the trade union leaders were intellectually unprepared to assume the role of social organizers.

The actual historical process was moving toward centralization and bureaucratic control, as indicated at that time by Trotsky's militarization of labor initiative as an early edition of Stalinism. The imperceptible metamorphosis of a disappointed radical and the surfacing of a new bourgeois from the revolutionary cocoon is not better illustrated than by Trotsky's assessment of labour unions: "The young socialist state requires trade unions, not for a struggle for better conditions of labour...but to organize the working class for the ends of production, to educate, discipline...to exercise their authority hand in hand with the state in order to lead the workers into the framework of a single economic plan."[8] And further on the methods recommended were: "measures of compulsion," the deprivation of the unions' autonomy, and the acceptance of an inevitable bureaucratization of the system, as the only way toward socialism "in a land of backward peasants and indifferent workers."[9]

The political concept of the fascist corporate state aimed for the same results, but with the difference that fascism preferred the outright destruction of the labor unions while Trotsky saw the goal being reached by the submission and manipulation of the workers' organizations.

Stalin cannot be blamed for inventing the politics of compulsion for the benefit of an omnipotent state. The theoretical elements, such as the dictatorship of the proletariat, and the empirical ones, such as the acute need for an efficient, highly organized apparatus to deal with the social-economic transformation, were already in place and many, like Trotsky, were unconsciously prodding in that direction a Bolshevik Party that still identified itself with socialist idealism.

One of the first manifestations of the move toward centralization was the creation of the Central Committee for Transport (Tsektran), under Trotsky's auspices. It was a compound of party, unions, and state organizations. The reaction to this measure was sharp and it was protested both inside the Communist Party, by the ultra-left, and by the unions, which sensed the gradual loss of their autonomy. The dissent reached its climax when the protagonists lined up in a clear demarcation of their ideological lines. On the one hand were Trotsky and Bukharin (still a leftist) who favored a centralized government of the economy, and on the other were Shliapnikov and Osinsky, who wanted unionist management of the economic reconstruction. The rift became more serious when the union supporters extended the factionalism from theoretical debate to organizational measures in their attempt to establish "an independent center of control over the Communist Party organizations in the trade unions."[10]

It was natural that the Leninists supported Trotsky's centralism despite their professed moderate attitude. When the Ninth Congress of the Communist Party endorsed the Leninist line the members of the workers' opposition appealed directly to the party membership.[11] Daniels points out that the oppositionist group enlisted "a considerable number of genuinely proletarian communist leaders, mostly in the trade unions: Shliapnikov, the first commissar of labor, and Lutovinov and S. Medvedev, the leaders of the metal workers, were preeminent. "The only important exception to the rule of worker-Bolshevik undergrounders was Alexandra Kollontai, aristocratic intellectual and former Menshevik emigré...."[12]

These actions may indicate that this particular controversy meant more than the usual ideological squabbles between the intellectual revolutionary leaders of the party; it may well suggest a first rift between the intellectual and worker elements of the revolution, at a time when the revolution was drifting away from the interests of the proletariat.

The Workers' Opposition crystallized in late 1920 and early 1921, in preparation for the Tenth Party Congress. Here they reasserted their position that: "The organization of the administration of the economy belongs to the All-Russian Congress of Producers, united in trade production unions, who elect the central organs which administer the whole economy of the Republic."[13] But the workers' disappointment with the direction which the party resolution was taking is best illustrated in a statement by the main ideologue of the workers' opposition, Alexandra Kollontai:

> The higher we go up the ladder of the Soviet and party hierarchy, the fewer adherents of the Opposition we find. The deeper we penetrate into the masses the more response do we find to the program of the workers' opposition....If the masses go away from the 'upper'; if there appears a break, a crack, between the directing centers and the 'lower' elements that means that there is something wrong with the 'upper' elements.[14]

These views reflected the strong utopianism and naiveté of the extreme left wing of the revolution, which still believed that the revolution must bring to power the working class. Being fully imbued with Marxist doctrine they were able to judge the situation only from a Marxist perspective. For them the biggest danger was represented by the bureaucratization process which was enveloping all the institutions of the revolution and which they attributed to the "petty bourgeois" influence which had penetrated the movement both physically and ideologically.

They were unable to see that neither the petty bourgeois influence nor bureaucratization represented the real danger to their illusions. It was rather the historical circumstances and necessity which empowered the best qualified social group to be the reorganizers of society; and that group, at that time, was not the proletariat but the intellectual revolutionaries. There was really no danger of outside bourgeois influence when all of the revolutionaries themselves were slowly becoming bourgeois. In retrospect, one realizes now the irreversibility of that process. No egalitarian measures borrowed from the experience of the Paris Commune that aimed at elevating the proletariat to the decision-making level and at compelling the revolutionary leaders to perform physical labor would have halted this process.

Ideologically the showdown between the revolutionary intellectuals on the left and right of the party's political spectrum came in the fall of 1920 when the Leninist line was adopted and the Workers' Opposition suppressed. Physically, the proletariat was reminded of its social status with the crushing of the Kronstadt revolt on March 2, 1921. After that the masses were silenced for good and the only opposition to the Leninist-Stalinist line came from the also dwindling groups of dissenting leaders. By that time, though, this dissent was motivated more by personal ambition than by ideological commitment.

The essence of the political ferment that had taken place was the conscious or unconscious realization that, in the long run, those who control the economy also control the politics. Although the contenders aimed at different goals the results would have been fairly similar no matter which side had won. The Workers' Opposition envisioned the takeover of the industrial administration by the unions with an administrative apparatus elected by and responsible to the organized workers. According to Daniels: "This meant the reorganization of the unions along lines similar to those envisaged by Trotsky, into 'production trade unions,' and the administration of the whole economy would be concentrated in their hands."[15]

Trotsky's plan called for a total merger of the trade unions and the state industrial administration in order to eliminate parallelism and confusion for the benefit of efficiency and centralism.

The end result of both processes would have been the same: centralization, either on party or union lines. The union's "productive democracy" would surely not have lasted long anyway due to its obvious anarchism and inefficiency. What was really at stake was the question of which group would be in charge of organizing the merger, because that group was to set the tone in both industry and politics. In Trotsky's variant the state would have absorbed the unions and imposed its rules over the workers. A victory by the unions would not have meant the gradual atrophy of the state, as Marxism expected, but the transformation of the unions into organs of the state.

The Leninist line was somewhere in the middle of this dispute, with a strong bent toward Trotsky's side. This came naturally because both policies were aimed at centralization and monopolization of power for the Communist Party, while the unionist stand, at best, was for a "separation of powers between party, the Soviets and the trade unions,"[16] as the unionist Shliapnikov suggested. This proposition was vehemently rejected by Lenin who stated, "The Russian Communist Party can in no case agree that political leadership alone should belong to the party, and economic leadership to the trade union. This is drawn from the views of the bankrupt second international."[17]

The Central Committee of the Communist Party met on November 8 and 9, 1920, to decide the party line on the issue and later on December 30, 1920, the trade union problem was vehemently discussed at the Eighth Congress of the Soviets. Although in both instances the Leninists voted against Trotsky and warned against the dangers of bureaucracy, overcentralization, and militarization, they remained faithful to the idea of centralization and union subordination to the party. It was during this period when the "transmission belt" theory crystallized the relationship between the Communist Party and the mass organizations. The Leninists, though, supported an attenuated form of centralization and took an ineffective stand on the issue of workers' democracy by proposing that the unions should function as a "shield for the workers against the possible abuses of 'state capitalism'."[18] All this was in order to avoid an estrangement of the unions when the party was still in need of their support. Nevertheless, the Central Committee voted a reform of the Tsektran instead of an outright dissolution of it as the unions demanded. It seems rather obvious that the divisiveness at that time, between Trotsky and the Leninists, was due to the fact that Trotsky came too early with his plan of state and party supremacy, the necessity of which was more than proven by the events that took place under Stalin's dictatorship.

The psychological separation between the working masses of proletarian and peasant background and the Communist Party came in March 1921. The realization that the regime was not going to surrender power, not even share it, came amid the torrent of bullets and blood of the Kronstadt revolt. The conflict brought to the surface the real sentiments of the new leaders and exposed the line they had drawn against proletarian hopes for social leadership.

Rightfully Daniels observed that:

> [in] the Kronstadt revolt,...factors of both proletarian and peasant unrest combined in an open challenge of Communist rule. Both repression and compromise were the response–compromise with the non-proletarian elements whose interests had suffered most under War Communism, but a campaign of extirpation against the critics on the Left, the revolution's most devoted partisans.[19]

The message of the Workers' Opposition reverberated through the discontented masses and ignited, through its counterpart, the Baltic Fleet Opposition, the Kronstadt revolt. The social makeup of the rebels consisted of workers and peasants serving the Soviet regime in the Baltic fleet. It is the view of this author that the disappointment of the masses over losing any hope for democratic participation in economic and social management was equal to if not stronger than their general discontent caused by economic distress and the severe damage done to their material interests by the policies of War Communism.

The essence of the revolt was precisely defined by Daniels when he wrote:

> Kronstadt was a movement of disillusioned revolutionaries, animated by the same kind of grievances expressed by the Ultra-Left Communists but outside the restraints of party loyalty and discipline. The Kronstadters revolted against the Soviet leaders in the name of the October Revolution itself.[20]

The violent reaction of the Soviet leaders, the branding of the revolution as a new White Guard plot, the wild and bloody suppression of the rebels, as well as the arrest of communist officials by the Kronstadters, indicates that both the toilers and the new leaders were already acting as separate classes, the first defending the ideals of the revolution, the second their newly acquired class interests.

The social cross section of those who participated in the suppression of the rebellion (Chekists, officer cadets from the Red Army training schools, top officials of the Communist Party sent directly from the halls of the Tenth Party Congress) indicates that the reliability of the members of the new class was still shaky and that only the top echelons could be trusted.

The opinion of some historians and communist leaders that the Kronstadt revolt could have been forestalled if the regime had instituted some corrective reforms[21] is not confirmed by subsequent events. The Kronstadt revolt may have been triggered by abuses of power but the real cause was the class differentiation toward which Soviet society was moving.

The class position taken by the rebels is well illustrated by the literature spread by the Kronstadters in which they spoke about a "third revolution" aimed at doing away with the "comissarocracy," whose aim they did not identify with.[22]

The suppression of the Kronstadt Revolt and the resolutions and directives issued by the Tenth Party Congress, based on the Leninist theory of party primacy and the recognition of the need for an avantgardist organization because of the proletariat's inability to rise above trade-union consciousness, opened the door to the full Stalinist implementation of the new class policy of centralization, statism, and regimentation.

But this policy was not a totally new phenomenon. Soon after the Bolshevik Revolution the communist ideal came into direct collision with everyday practice of managing the economic and social problems. If prior to the Revolution the communists sincerely believed that their ideal was the purest reflection of the workers' strivings, the reality of power brought them head on against the workers' interests. The traditional capitalist-worker relationship reappeared soon in the state-owned economy, although the consciousness of its reality crystallized slowly. It took decades, the struggles of the opposition inside the party, the opposition of trade unions against the party, and the confrontations between the workers and the communist state, till both the new leaders and the workers realized that they were on different sides of a fence. Many authors agree that the more evident signs of this separation of interests surfaced approximately at the same period in which the Communist Party estranged itself from the peasantry. What the collectivization of 1929 did to the peasants, the stress of the First Five Year Plan of 1928, did to the workers. Despite strong ideological qualms, Lenin had spelled out the need for labor unions to remain apolitical organizations. The party leadership, using the resolution of the Ninth Congress, stepped up its efforts to disarm the workers by transforming their only true proletarian organization into an agent of government.

> Under the dictatorship of the proletariat [stated the Resolution] the trade unions cease to be organizations which sell labor power to an employing class. There can be no question of trade union opposition to the institutions of the Soviet State. Such opposition is a deviation from Marxism to bourgeois trade unionism.[23]

This trend was reaffirmed by the Sixth Congress of the Communist Party in 1930, where the role of the trade unions was described in the following terms:

> Socialist competition in the shock brigades must becomes the primary

concern of all the constructive activities of the unions. The problem of the trade unions is the organization of socialist competition and the shock brigades.[24]

Slowly the Soviet worker was completely subdued into a situation resembling feudal servitude. Protection of labor became solely the management's concern, just as changing working places was done only with the management's approval. The worker became physically responsible to the management for the quantity and quality of his products and the integrity of the tools used. Since the amount of the wages paid was the concern only of management, productive quotas were rapidly increased and nominal salaries raised only slowly, which resulted in a net decrease of the real wages.

But this process was more far-reaching than a simple reaction to the political problems of the moment. In addition to suppressing their previous supporters, the workers, the political leaders were also making order in their own ranks, which were undergoing a process of formation.

Despite many divergences, especially on the issue of unions, in this new crisis the moderate left, represented by Trotsky and Bukharin, remained loyal to Lenin as did the Leninists during the Tsektran crisis. It seems that the general tendency toward centralism and authority was the basic platform around which the interests of the new class crystallized.

CHAPTER VI

CLASS POLICY AGAINST THE PEASANTRY

The more the Stalinist "third revolution" progressed, the more the real character of the new society was revealed. The separation of the producers from the means of production was a repeat, on a new social basis, of the old property concept. There was a new bourgeoisie with a new system of organization, who shared the profits deriving from the limited and collective class ownership of a nationalized industrial sector, which offered them the advantages of a concentrated economy without a formal property title over it. At the same time the private ownership in agriculture enjoyed a short renaissance during the NEP period, because of economic difficulties resulting from the failure of War Communism, and the necessity to forestall any attempt at expanding the new forms of ownership in agriculture for the fear of further estranging the peasant. All this in a period when the Soviet regime was not yet well established.

As the Communist leaders gained more political ground and felt more secure in their position of power, their attention became more and more concentrated on the agricultural sector of the economy.

I mentioned previously the complex and selective way in which Leninism treated the peasant question during different stages of the revolution. By and large Leninist theory supported the idea of collaboration and alliance with all the peasantry, with the exception of a thin layer of wealthy peasants. In Stalinist practice, though, the communist regime actually turned against the whole peasantry, imposing on them oppressive measures and discriminating against them with intensity. The question of what inspired such a policy is not easy to answer, although there have been multiple explanations. First of all, the largely accepted theory is that the oppression of the peasant strata was but another side of the same system that oppressed the industrial worker. This is acceptable in view of the regime's profile and its emphasis on industrialization rather than socialism. Therefore it seemed proper, in view of the sacrifices which the system demanded from them, to direct the brunt of oppression also against the worker and peasant and not only against the nationalized bourgeoisie. This theory is increasingly supported as against the view that the massive collectivization was the result of immediate economic difficulties derived from the excessive industrialization and the limited potential of the NEP policy to promote further development. Second, it appears that the Bolshevik Revolution reached a watershed with the completion of nationalization and securing of the political monopoly. While Marxist ideology was calling, at this stage of development, for a settled, relatively tranquil evolution toward socialist relations paralleled by the atrophy of state and party, the leaders found themselves in an awkward situation. On the one hand accustomed to the tempest of revolution, they saw in tranquil development, and in the workers' political inactivity, the possibility and dangers of a return to capitalism. On the other hand, the prospect of abdicating their newly gained power, and the increasing privileges that came with it, did not inspire their enthusiasm for social justice. The lull in the revolutionary tempest, represented by the NEP period, seems to have provoked some confusion among the party leaders as to which direction to steer the political events. The fact that the proletariat remained politically inert and basically oriented only to its immediate economic interests, and the Kronstadt experience of 1921 which separated the avantgardist party from the worker and peasant masses, brought the Bolshevik leaders to a crisis of identity. For this reason the surfacing of opposition groups inside the Bolshevik Party indicated not only a simple divergence of opinion over the politic-economic path to be followed toward power, but genuine anxieties over what would be possible and what would be necessary in future development. It seems that there was an acute need for new horizons, for a clear program of action which would affirm the legitimacy of the new leaders and their survival in power. When the Bolsheviks ran out of unfulfilled and unfulfillable promises inspired by Marxist theory, they had to come up with a concrete plan which would hold at least the promise of reaching a socialist goal. Quite naturally such a plan was to be a plan for economic development executed under a restructured framework of ownership, which would open for Bolsheviks new prospects. This plan would give them the opportunity to manipulate not only the industrialization process toward desired forms, but to apply a methodology for its fulfillment which would once and for all secure their political power and reduce the working masses to total submission. The phenomenon of uncertainty at first manifested itself in the form of personal conflict among the decision makers (the Leninists, the left and right opposition) over the policy to be followed, and by the end of the decade it finally took the form of a concrete shift from NEP policy to that of the "third revolution."

These events were similar to those in 1794 when the leaders of the French Revolution, after achieving their initial goals, brought Jacobin radicalism to a cul de sac. They tried in vain to solve the political impasse caused by a lack of new goals and programs on which to base their political activity. Suddenly their revolutionary idealism faced a stark reality which was impervious to any political ideal that did not directly advance the economic and political interest of the big entrepreneurs. Their strivings to give a new meaning to their activity by introducing a new calendar, a new moral code, etc. proved to be superficial and alien to the majority of the bourgeoisie, who were by that time interested only in bringing France back to the normalcy of uneventful business activity.

The revolutionary leaders did not understand that their role as agents of transformation actually had ended, together with their idealistic dreams, and that it was time to cede the leadership to the actual masters: *la grande bourgeoisie.*

The importance of uncertainty and intuition is also acknowledged by M. Lewin when he assigns to the grain crisis in Russia more a role as catalyst than as generator of the collectivization policy and other radical measures in 1929.[1] He states:

> No one had yet dreamed of mass collectivization as a rapid and effective means of solving both current and long-term problems at one and the same time. The plan was ratified by the Congress of Soviets in May 1929. The great majority of the party leadership did not, either at this stage or in the autumn, foresee what decisions were to be taken some six months later.[2]

Lewin ascribes the "third revolution" to the general economic failures and the need for radical changes in agriculture in order to avoid any jeopardy to industrialization,[3] but while this explanation can be accepted, like his reference to the grain crisis, in terms of denoting a catalyst, it does not explain the intensity, the speed, or the determination of the communist action in collectivization and "dekulakization." Only a more profound motivation among party leaders, like the intuitively felt necessity to extend a restricted form of collective ownership in agriculture as a guarantee of the perpetuation of the same form of ownership in industry, can fully account for their actions.

The method used in implementing the new forms of ownership was also significant. It was the method of violent, revolutionary action, in order to perpetuate the psychology of revolutionary change so strongly identified with the circumstances in which the new leaders came to power. It might appear that the development of a comparatively calm, business-like period would be perceived by the communist leaders as a threat to their situation, which was acquired and accustomed in the storm of revolution. By October 1929 the stage was finally set for complete collectivization, as "Pravda" stated in unequivocal terms.[4] This political offensive by the leadership could be a border line which marks the transformation of the new leaders from a "class by itself" into a "class for itself."

Taking a retrospective view of the post revolutionary period, it appears that the economic imbalance caused by an overtaxed industrial system, the failure of the NEP to work in an environment still full of restraints, and the seeming necessity of collectivizing agriculture in order to reestablish the economic balance between agriculture and industry, were circumstances through which the new form of capitalist property was taken shape.

The crystallization process which brought the new class to the surface was almost instantly followed by the return of social inequality. Although full equality was never implemented in post revolutionary Russia, an apparent equalization process had emerged briefly during the revolutionary strife and the civil war. But soon after, military actions subdued this move and a return to normalcy became imperative, the procapitalist measures of the NEP period brought back economic inequalities. These inequalities proved to be short lived ones and qualitatively different from the social and economic inequalities which grew out of the communist regime itself. Different segments of the Soviet society received differentiated treatment, and the differences in social standing and life style became greater and greater between those who labored and those who organized. More important, the differences that manifested themselves in actual life became consciously accepted. Money, commerce, personal ambition, and achievement, hitherto associated with capitalism, became again appreciated factors. On the other hand, equality of needs and of opportunity became the object of disdain and was branded as "petty bourgeois manifestations." Differences in social status became manifest in the army, in the factory, on farms and offices, as David J. Dallin rightly pointed out in his book "The Real Russia":

A new period began with the second Soviet revolution–the sweeping industrialization and collectivization. The instructions given from above were, 'Down with equalitarianism!' Those who attempted to resist were ruthlessly eliminated. In his conflict with the left-wing factions, Stalin frequently denounced in sharp terms the 'nonsense that money was unnecessary' and trade was a 'dead letter.' He assailed the demand for social equality by dubbing it ironically the *uravnilovka*–contemptuous Russian slang for equalitarianism.[5]

The old story repeated itself. Those individuals who were able to combine ability with ruthlessness were making their way to the top echelons of the new order. Those who were endowed only with ability and were unable to shake off the heavy weight of illusions had to clear the scene, like Michael Tomsky, leader of the Soviet trade unions, whose only remedy for his shattered dreams was suicide.

It was not actually a new system, but rather the old capitalism with new form and meaning. Similarly, the new leaders resembled in many ways the old bourgeoisie, although they were a new breed with a different philosophy and different relations and allegiances among themselves.

Again Dallin was right when he stated:

> The new aristocracy *in spe* won its rights by labor and sacrifice; it was the more reminiscent of those ancient conquerors from whom, through storm and stress, stemmed the future lords, junkers, and noblemen, than of the modern men of property.[6]

The central aim toward which the society was striving and the new morality which was molded to support those strivings had little in common with the idea of social justice. It was concepts of industrialization, of converging capital and labor, of expediency, efficiency, of planning, which preoccupied the new leaders, and their real interest was expressed in outlets ranging from primitive forms of propaganda to sophisticated manifestations of art and literature. The Stalin era is the time in which not only did the ideal and ideas of the new class find their expression but the social origins of the new leaders became more evident. As the formative process was still at its beginning stages, the cross section of the new class was not yet fully crystallized.

CHAPTER VII

THE SOURCE OF POWER: BUREAUCRACY VERSUS POLITICAL LEADERS

The critical period for the revolution, the year 1921, marked the start of a triple process of centralization and control, involving the state over the masses, the party over the state, and the individual over the party. The parallelism of these processes reflects the predominant concept of the new leaders: intensive centralization and subordination of all state and party organizations to a small group of policy makers for the sake of rationalization and efficiency. Later the concept of centralization would serve not only to promote the idea of efficiency but to defend the class interests of the new leaders. Both in society and party the shape of the new feudalistic pyramid of power and influence was taking form. As Daniels pointed out:

> ...the organizational structure of the party evolved rapidly toward bureaucratic perfection, rounding out a trend that had begun during the Civil War. The Soviets, nominally the organs of local government, lost power to the party; local organizations, including those in the party, lost authority to central organizations. Large parliamentary bodies lost authority to smaller committees.[1]

On each level of the party, the secretary nominally elected by the corresponding committee but actually nominated by the central secretariat,[2] concentrated the power in his own hands. Their allegiance was not directed, therefore, toward the masses or the nominating committee but toward the central organization. A particular relationship between the party cadres on the different levels of power evolved. The regional secretaries, nominated and supported by the central authority, had an unwritten obligation to manipulate the party delegates selected for the election of the central authorities in order to secure their reelection. Applying this system at all party levels secured the permanency of the leadership, especially in the higher echelons of the party. A clear *seigneur* and vassal relationship developed in party life. A similar reconstructing of power took place in all the institutions and state apparatus of Soviet society. Stalin, an apparatchnik par excellence owed his increasing power to this evolving mechanistic, structural politics. The implementation of this new political orientation was facilitated by the fact that the process, though new in essence, was not unfamiliar to the Russian masses in form. The tsarist autocracy through the centuries habituated the Russians to a blind subordination and respect for the authority of state and monarchy. Because the Bolshevik ideologues conditioned the construction of socialism on industrialization, which in turn hinged on the existence of a highly selective and centralized state, the existence of a hierarchal bureaucracy to run that system became indispensable. The formation of the new bureaucracy enabled a special group of people, able and willing to adapt themselves to the new economic and political requirements, to become agents of the transformation process unleashed by the revolutionary leaders. To be sure, as in the case of all bureaucracies, there was the looming danger that these agents of transformation would tend to pervert their role as executors of policy into that of decision makers.

Although not a socialist invention, the bureaucracy in the Soviet case became an ever increasing and all enveloping administrative structure. Unlike the previous stage of capitalism when the bureaucracy was made up only of state enforcement agencies, now, due to the state form of ownership, it extended also into the productive system. In the Soviet Union the state bureaucracy showed an overwhelming increase from 1 million government employees at the time of the revolution to 2,500,000 in 1926, to over 28 million after World War II.[3]

Like many other authors, Dallin suggests that the bureaucracy forming the backbone of the new class was in fact the power source of this class. But while it is true that in modern times, the bureaucracy with its distinctive size has exerted power and influence by itself, it never became the source of decision making and power. It was rather the vehicle of power, the means of implementing the whims and decisions of a relatively small group of leaders.

This observation is emphasized by Rudolph Hilferding, a leader of the prewar German Social Democratic Party and a leading theorist of Marxism. Hilferding rightly observes that the bureaucracy in the new society remained only the implementing instrument of those leaders who actually retained state power, whom he narrows down to a small circle at the top level of the Communist Party.

His argument is based on the theory that the bureaucracy, without the policy maker, plays a special regulating role in a system which is neither capitalist nor socialist and which he calls totalitarian. It is not capitalist because the nationalization of the means of production radically altered the economic structure, destroying, although not completely, the free market and transforming the system from a market economy into a consumer economy. It is not socialist because "socialism is indissolubly linked to democracy," which is totally absent from the new system. Furthermore, socialization did not free the economy from the rule of one class in order to vest that rule in society as a whole.[4] In the new system it was the state planning commission (a segment of the bureaucracy) that determined what was to be produced and how, and not the price incentives of the free market system. This direct interference of the state into the economic activity and lives of the producers made the new system a unique form of totalitarianism. In Hilferding's view, prices and wages, which did not disappear, had only a limited role in determining the share of the particular services from the total products which the state allocated for consumption.

Hilferding's observations relating to the totalitarian aspect of Soviet socialism, although true in general, fail to pinpoint the social forces behind the totalitarian state. His theory focuses on an impersonal all-powerful state which hovers over all social classes, oppressing them with equal perseverance, if not equal severity. Under this state power the new forms of social distribution, revolutionary as they might be, still did not change the basic dichotomous and unequal structure of society, but continued to be restrictive toward the masses and more liberal toward the leaders.

Placing the source of power and policy making in the bureaucracy leads only to confusion by reducing the role of the political leadership to that of executors and elevating the huge machinery of bureaucracy to the exalted position of decision maker. This interpretation fails to define the Soviet bureaucracy in its proper dimensions as subordinated to the political power yet with an ever increasing size and role in administering the expanding system of production and distribution as a special body at the center of the whole industrial complex.

In Hilferding's vision the totalitarian state becomes an independent power "subjecting social forces and compelling them to serve its ends," and "the totalitarian power lives by the economy, but not for the economy or even for the class ruling the economy as in the case of the bourgeois state."[5] But to be overwhelmed by the awesome power of the state, means in an indirect way to recognize the independent power of the bureaucracy, and to see it as the embodiment of the state. In doing this he contradicts what he had said a few lines earlier, that it was impossible for bureaucracy to become the social ruler due to its heterogeneous makeup.

> Bureaucracy everywhere [writes Hilferding] and particularly in the Soviet Union, is composed of a conglomeration of the most varied elements. To it belong not only government officials in the narrow sense of the word (i.e., from minor employees up to the generals and even Stalin himself) but also the directors of all branches of industry and such functionaries as, for example, the postal and railway employees.[6]

Although the bureaucracy is only an administrative structure for the implementation of policy, its importance should not be discounted. In the Soviet Union, the bureaucracy was entrusted with, among other things, the reorganization and reconstruction of the economy. In his work "The Immediate Tasks of the Soviet Regime," Lenin emphasized the need for an "orderly administration and effective control over both capitalist and nationalized enterprises." Because the Soviet bureaucracy is today still in a relatively early period of its development, it is hard to make a precise assessment of its future role. It is still unclear whether the Soviet bureaucracy will eventually merge with the leading political group, forming a monolithic power structure, remain only an executor of directives, or perhaps overwhelm the political leaders due to the expanding role of the managerial technocracy. Despite the fact that the bureaucracy, and for that matter the political leadership itself, is still open to a continuous replenishing of its ranks from below, it cannot claim to have a proletarian essence. Notwithstanding the gradual replacement of the old bureaucratic and entrepreneurial personnel with new elements of peasant and worker origin, the general social structure has remained the same: a dichotomous social cross section with producers on one hand and leaders on the other. The proletarian elements which still enrich the political leadership and bureaucracy loses its old class awareness and very quickly identifies themselves with the new power structure. The numerous tendencies and habits of the old bourgeoisie, borrowed and displayed by the new power elite, are rapidly assimilated by the newcomers.

Their eagerness to secure a particular lifestyle, which sets them apart from the masses, and their acquisition of academic degrees and distinctions, rapidly transforms the selected ex-workers into a fully-grown bourgeois.

The essence of the Soviet state, the bureaucracy, and leading political groups was analyzed by Marcuse, whose opinion on this matter is: "...domination remains a specialized function in the division of labor and is as such the monopoly of a political, economic, and military bureaucracy."[7] As to the relationship between the bureaucracy and the political leaders, he emphasizes the importance of the leaders of the centralized authoritarian organization, who rule outside "the collective control of the ruled population."[8] But while Marcuse observes a clear distinction between producers and administrators, he comes to no conclusion as to whether the administrators and policy makers form, together or separately, a historical class.

Marcuse denies the class character of both the bureaucracy and the political leaders if the issue is defined in terms of their relationship to the means of production, that is, in terms of ownership. If the issue is approached from the point of view of control over the means of production, the answer depends on whether such control is effectively in the hands of the "immediate producers."[9] The obvious reality in Soviet political life is that the population never delegated power and control to the leaders; on the contrary, the power was slowly arrogated by a small minority. This concentration of control among bureaucrats and political leaders gives credence to the argument that this groups forms a separate class from the rest of the population.[10] Marcuse reinforces this conclusion when he writes:

> ...if the bureaucracy were open to ascent 'from below,' it would still be a class as long as the separatedness of its function made it independent from the people whom it manages and administers.[11]

Marcuse recognizes that "bureaucracy does not generate self-perpetuating power unless it has an economic base of its own."[12] And, because bureaucracy does not own the means of production and neither do the political leaders, two questions arise: Who owns the means of production? and Does control over the means of production generate a base strong enough to replace the individual ownership?

In the new economic setup, ownership seems to have been replaced by political power (control over the means of production), which proves to be sufficient to secure the smooth working of the economy. State ownership appears to be the nominal solution in a situation where individual ownership has become obsolete and society is still not ready for collective public ownership. In such conditions the concept of ownership becomes superfluous.

As for the relationship between the bureaucracy and the political leaders, Marcuse differentiates between technical-administrative and social control. He points out that according to Soviet doctrine, the party, which exercises social control, has the ability to override technical-administrative control.[13] This places the political leaders in a position of clear superiority over the bureaucracy and suggests a process of qualitative differentiation in which two social forces tend to cluster in amicable but separate groups. To be sure, from a historical point of view such a separation can be viable only if the leading class is able to fulfill the requirements of economic and technological development. But to this we will return later.

The expanded role of the bureaucracy evolved amid a growing clash between the concepts of collegial and individual leadership and management. Barrington Moore points to the decreasing role of collegial management which even in its flourishing period during the Civil War was merely "an extreme manifestation"[14] and the epitome of inefficiency. This process had already begun in 1919, with the decrease in size of the collegiums which included, besides the workers, an increasing number of engineers and technicians approved by the trade unions. When these collegiums did not satisfy the requirements of efficiency, the individual responsibility became prevalent. Although during the 1920s there were some vacillations between the two concepts of management, the last strong appeal for collegial management, as the sole avenue of mass participation in administering industry and the society, was made in 1920 by Tomsky, a trade-union leader and a member of the Workers' Opposition.

Barrington Moore considers the Ninth and Eleventh Party congresses as the turning point which saw an end to any involvement of the labor unions in the problems of management.[15] The subsequent step, the creation of the "triangle" formed by the factory management, the party cell, and the union, lasted well into the 1930s but also proved unsatisfactory due to the continuous struggle for influence among the three groups.

This competition for a dominant position in the administration may have been an ominous sign of things to come. At the time of the Twelfth Party Congress some managerial groups gathered around Krassin and criticized the party for lacking good managers. It is said that Krassin "complained that the top party leaders were the same as they had been two decades previously, 'newspaper dilettantes and litterateurs!'"[16] There is a strong possibility that the revolutionary changes, started in February 1917 and continued in October 1917, and further extended in 1929 in the form of the Stalinist revolution, might not even have ended yet. The revolutionary leaders whom Krassin pointedly described as dilettantes and litterateurs, whose sophisticated and idealist intellectualism inspired revolutionary changes at the social level, might have been unable, precisely because of their total absorption in revolutionary theory, to comprehend the cold and stern realities of technical and business management. By and large a technocrat is not a revolutionary and a revolutionary is seldom a technocrat. The political leaders' inability to see that their actions serve less and less the interests of the workers and more and more those of the strata which enjoys the major share of the benefits accruing from social production and industrialization, makes them an increasing liability for the movement which they initiated. It may be that in the future, the managers, technical specialists, and other administrators of the economy will challenge the political leaders for the exalted position which they have held and enjoyed so much.

CHAPTER VIII

THE SOURCE OF INDIVIDUAL POWER

The tremendous development of the Soviet bureaucracy cannot be attributed solely to administrative-technical problems in need of continuous solutions. The growing bureaucracy also reflected those social stratifications which Soviet society underwent during the Stalin era and has continued to undergo till the present time. Despite its practical and theoretical subordination to the political leadership, the centralized and hierarchial bureaucracy imposed itself on the revolutionary leadership, which was motivated by democratic-ideological principles, but succumbed to the bureaucratic principle of personal rule. Yet the roots of power still are not embedded in personal rule, powerful though it may be. In Marcuse's opinion:

> Personal power, even if effectively institutionalized, does not define social control. Stalin's dictatorship may well have overridden all divergent interests by virtue of his factual power. However, this personal power was itself subject to the requirements of the social system on whose continued functioning it depended.[1]

In other words the whims of the ruler are curtailed by the class interests he represents, which in turn are determined by objective needs of socio-economic function and development. But, in the Soviet case, Marcuse does not find "any homogeneous group to which social control could be meaningfully attributed.[2] He finds, though, two forces which forestall the complete monopolization of power: the Central Plan and the competitive terror.

Marcuse, searching for the roots of power, must return again to the bureaucracy, specifically to its major branches: government, party, armed forces, management.3 This seemingly confusing approach which attributes and also denies to the bureaucracy the roots of power, and regards the political leadership as also subordinated to its own terroristic dictatorship, can be explained perhaps by the fact that the new ruling class is still in a formative stage in which the ruling power, although monopolized by the political leadership, is not yet firmly established but is still subject to external challenges and internal instability. This situation gives rise to the hazy quality of Soviet political life, in which the roots of state power, though omnipresent, are hard to define.

There is some evidence of reciprocity between the totalitarian bureaucracy and the dictatorship by the individual in the society administered by such a bureaucratic system. Perhaps the rigidly centralized form of bureaucracy, which excludes the expression of mass opinion for the sake of smooth and efficient administration is partially responsible for the growth of a system that requires the seemingly autocratic rule of the individual. Although far from being a perfect mechanism, a totalitarian bureaucracy run by an individual still has the advantage over a democracy when it comes to the rapidity of decision making and implementation. This is, perhaps, why a totalitarian system has always exhibited, besides a well-developed bureaucracy, the uncontested rule of a dictator.

In many cases, including Stalin's, the personality of the dictator has attracted more attention than the historical function he was fulfilling. There is a great deal of written material which ascribes to Stalin's cruel personality, his ruthlessness and egomania, and the political excesses he committed against the Soviet population. Isaac Deutscher, in his book *From Stalin: A Political Biography,* considers Stalin's lack of strong personality, his relative anonymity, as assets for his ascendancy to power. He also emphasizes Stalin's strategic position in the party leadership as the First Secretary and the only permanent liaison officer between the Politburo and the Orgbureau, his permanent contact with the living body of the party, and his ability and opportunity to manipulate the party's cadres in behalf of his own interest. As Deutscher correctly observed, a dualism of authority slowly evolved in the top echelons of the party in which the Politburo, despite its formal organizational superiority and its exalted position as the personification of the Bolshevik spirit, more and more became dependent on "the more material power of management and direction" of the General Secretariat.[4] The old Bolshevik guard like Trotsky, Zinoviev, Kamenev, Bukharin, were constituted a highly sophisticated brand of intellectuals who were attracted to the revolution due to reason and humanitarianism inspired precisely by their intellectuality. But inside this type of *l'homme rationnel* more often than not lurked an astonishing political *naiveté* which, in the quotidian clashes of programs and personalities, proved to be a dangerous liability in comparison with the earthy, clever, often unprincipled but realistically practical stand of the Stalinists. But these practical advantages of the Stalinist group still do not explain their tremendous and speedy success in disposing of the opposition and enslaving the party. This process cannot be explained simply on the basis of a ruthless personality and organized ability. Stalin must have had the support of the majority of the leading class in his campaign of political terror even if that terror was partially directed against them. It was in their interest to support a government of iron discipline as sure safeguard for their newly acquired privileges. Instinctively they must have felt that the new form of ownership which made available to them a disproportionate share of the national product had to be embedded in a system distantly resembling feudalism, a framework of severe and strictly defined obligations that citizens owed to the party and to the state. Stalin also must have realized that while the old bourgeoisie was able to act politically through organized individual votes, the new class of leaders was able to express itself only through its supreme organizational form: the party. He must have realized the advantages of this system and at the same time the possibility of keeping the party under control. It was exactly this reality on which Stalin rested his political scheme while his opponents built their policies on the chimera of ideology. In other words it was not only Stalin's ambition to reach the zenith of power that made him the absolute dictator over Soviet politics, but also the circumstances which allowed, even demanded, such ambition to be successful.

In many revolutions, sooner or later the revolutionary leadership breaks up into several groups due to differences in personality and opinions, and to a divergence over the assessment of the general social and political trends. The clash between different groups within the Soviet Communist Party was due by and large to the abovementioned reasons. While the showdown with the left opposition seems to have been motivated mainly by personality differences, the showdown with the right appears to have been a matter of profound policy disagreements.

When a crucial point in revolutionary development is reached, a point usually manifested by a political or economic crisis which needs an urgent solution, in the case of the Soviet Union the grain crisis and the declining success of the NEP policy, divergent groups move to implement their programs on the basis of their perception of the situation. Usually the victors in the clash which follows are not only the most opportunist and ruthless but also those whose program reflects the conscious and unconscious desires and interests of the new class in ascension.

It appears that in the Soviet context too, because the new class had neither the juridical nor historical justification for its social hegemony and since from the beginning of the Russian Revolution of 1917 their sole justification as leaders of the movement had been their ability to ride high the revolutionary tide, a new socio-economic upheaval would give them a second opportunity to demonstrate their social utility and at the same time choose a program that would both promote their inherent interests and provide the avenue to solving the immediate crisis. The new class had to choose the Stalinist faction because it actually had the ruthless efficiency needed to solve the crisis in a dynamic way and put an end to the NEP period which in their perception was leading to a "return to capitalism." As long as it is clear that the third revolution's principal aim was industrialization and the further centralization of the economy, collectivization being a part of that strategy and a vehicle to achieve it, it must also be recognized that such a policy coincided completely with the historical role of the new class. The new leaders appeared more and more defined as the agent of the second industrialization and not of socialism. This became clear in the Stalinist positions toward general issues of policy, and in the leaders' statements and actions.[5]

There should be no doubt in anyone's mind that the evolution of Stalinism was the result of significant social changes that had already begun during the February Revolution and perhaps even before. It was the result of necessary structural changes that mainly affected the upper levels of a society which was to perpetuate capitalist production relations amid new circumstances and with new managerial methodology. From such a perspective, Stalinism cannot be viewed as a historical accident or an overmanifestation of subjectivism as Roy Medvedev suggests when he criticizes those writers who consider the phenomenon of Stalinism as the result of an objective socio-economic process.[6] Those writers were right when they concluded that Stalin fit the circumstances and did not create those circumstances. It is true, however, that "Stalinism" could have been either a milder or even worse form of dictatorship depending on the person who played Stalin's role. But it is certain that the historical circumstances required an authoritarian system to fulfill the requirements of the new historical situation and carry out the will of the new class representing this new situation. Furthermore, only an authoritarian system was capable of solving the economic crisis through which these circumstances manifested themselves. How can one reject the inevitability of Stalinism when the development of most socialist or protosocialist countries has taken the form of party or military dictatorship with, in most cases, a single dictator in charge.

Medvedev was right when he detected a relationship between Stalin's violence and his popularity. True, it was a popularity achieved through a daily and persistent outpouring of personality propaganda, but it also was a genuine popularity inspired by the class interests of the party, state, and technical bureaucrats who saw in Stalin's regime not only the security of their privileged position but also the avenue to further development of a highly concentrated, super-technological economy and administration, of which they believed it to be a portent. Medvedev sees new elements rising above the communist consciousness, the elements of professional, institutional, and personal dedication, but he attributes all these to a freaky deviation from the communist principles, many of which he finds are surviving the Stalinist autocracy,[7] and not to the objective existence of new social forces and exigencies evolving in Soviet society.

In conclusion it may be said that Stalinism was a logical continuation of Leninism, not only in the sense that it followed the basic Leninist principles calling for an avantgardist leadership over the proletariat, that it accepted the continuing existence of the state, the preservation of the political monopoly of the Communist Party, in the country at large, the liquidation of any kind of opposition, and the preservation of a monolithic leadership inside the organization, but also because it led to those logical outcomes, as a consequence of the general Leninist policies, which Lenin himself would have been compelled to pursue. It was such outcomes as the abandonment of democratic principles on which the new society was to be built, the nonrealization of social hegemony of the proletariat, and the demise of egalitarian principles in assigning the roles in production and in the distribution of goods, which contradicted most Marxist principles concerning a socialist environment. These outcomes in their innermost quality meant the radical and permanent separation of the revolutionaries from the workers which presumably Lenin did not expect but was simply acknowledged by Stalinist practice. The fact that Stalin emphasized some aspects of Leninist theory and neglected others was not the result of a conscious intention to deviate from Leninism but rather the desire to match the theory to the actual needs of political expediency. For Stalin it was not hard to deviate from time to time from explicit or implicit Leninist prescriptions and at the same time remain Leninist. It was the essence of Leninist thought, inspired by a compelling reality, that inadvertently put the Communist Party in the awkward position of being a dominating instead of an equalizing agent.

The changes from the Leninist line brought about by Stalinist policy run deep. If these changes are less noticeable in the theoretical domain, they are more obvious in those concrete results produced by the combination of Leninist theory and Stalinist implementation.

It was precisely during the Stalinist period that Marxist-Leninist expectations of socialism were confronted by the stern reality that it would be impossible to achieve in the present historical period anyway. The void left by the disintegration of the socialist dream was soon filled by those careerist elements eager to carve out a position in the new economic organization where common interests and preoccupations, as organizers of production, forged them into a new entrepreneurial class.

It cannot be said that the changes in the official policy of the Communist Party and its effects on class relations were totally different from the reality which Lenin bequeathed to Stalin. There remained the same dichotomous social setup which the revolution tried but was unable to abolish. The only major change, that in the upper levels of society, had been achieved with the seizure of power by the Bolsheviks in October 1917, and only perfected by the Stalinists. The political leadership refused to hand power over to the proletariat, and the proletariat would have been unable to receive it even if it had been offered. The permanency of this situation was a fact which became more and more obvious in the Stalin era.

Stalin did not really bring innovations and new orientation to Leninism. That was not really needed. Leninism already contained those elements useful for a social class which has in mind to build a corporate state for the sake of an overall effort to industrialize and adapt the country to the needs of a technological society. Most of Stalin's writings are simplifications and even vulgarizations of Marxist and Leninist thoughts. If the early writings of Stalin contained a mixture of Menshevism and

Leninism, the later writings were apologetics for the conformism to Leninism of the measures which the Communist Party took in its internal and external policies under Stalin's administration.

Stalin's seminarist mind, habituated to absolute categories, was instinctively attracted to that part of Leninism that was devoted to rigid organizational schemes.

It was not so much the obsession with power, in a lesser degree with Lenin and a higher degree with Stalin, which made them successful, but the objective needs of a socio-economic development which required a strong personality to harness all the social resources for rapid change in the economic structure and to help mold a group made up half of revolutionaries and half of careerist elements into a new class of leaders. This group was unable to do that task by itself without an adequate economic basis to unify them, an economic base which they had to create in order to survive as a new class of entrepreneurs.

Stalin did not really separate the organization from the socialist ideal. There was nothing to separate. The organization was something concrete, real, something to deal with, while the socialist ideal was nothing more than its name suggested: an abstract concept.

The continuing existence and growth, after the revolution, of the state machinery, meant for Lenin a temporary stewardship by the state to allow time to educate and elevate the proletariat to a level of statesmanship that would enable it to fulfill its historical mission. For Stalin the state became an end of itself, a means to protect class interests, a place where the new leaders could rally and organize themselves. If Stalin enslaved the working class through the five-year plans and the peasantry through the collectivization of agriculture, he only continued what Lenin started when he refused the working class participation in government through a coalition of worker's parties and labor unions as was suggested by the railway unions immediately after the revolution.

Stalin's measures to control every facet, every life expression of the working class, were but a logical conclusion to the outlawing of almost all working-class and peasant parties during

Lenin's administration. Stalinism was the result of a new era opened by the Russian Revolution of 1917, which introduced new relations among the old and new social classes of Russia. These relations were based on totalitarianism and the submission to the will of the collective both by the lower classes and the leaders. Personal freedom, so characteristic of the anarchical stage of capitalism, was exchanged for a more or less tolerable regimentation of the individual along with a relative security of material existence. Although it is presently still manifested through the charismatic leadership of a dictator, there are strong indications that the collective dictat and centralization will prevail in the distant future under the control of a new entrepreneurial intelligentsia.

CHAPTER IX

OTHER ALTERNATIVES TO EMPIRICAL SOCIALISM

Of the numerous problems targeted by Marxism only a very few were selected for analysis in the present work, namely, those deemed the most obvious deviations from Marxist doctrine, and which bear the utmost consequences both for empirical socialism and the theory which tried to explain it. Issues such as the dictatorship of the proletariat, the gradual atrophy and disappearance of the repressive features of the state, the communist regime's policy toward the industrial working class and peasantry, the internal development of the Communist Party from its professed proletarian character to an instrument of suppression of the proletariat, the economic policies of the Communist parties after the conquest of power, and the gradual decline of Marxist doctrine, were the central points of this undertaking. The above elements, actually, but not formally, deviated from the expected path to socialism. This deviation was a result, not only of the narrow-minded and rigid policy of the communist regime, in which necessary empirical deviations from doctrine were not matched by a theoretical flexibility to remold the doctrine to historical reality, but also of the inapplicability of many Marxian tenets to the situation that existed after the revolution. For this reason any attempt to revitalize the doctrine had to come either from outside the Communist bloc or from individuals who formally or informally divorced themselves from the socialist movement.

Besides the empirical shortcomings of the Communist parties in applying and updating the theory, Marxism suffered from structural deficiencies such as the strong influence of normative elements and revolutionary passions. Such limitations hindered Marxism from making a realistic evaluation of the laboring classes, the limits of their possibilities as elements of change, and the timing for the advent of socialism. It may be said that although Marxism achieved significant results in analyzing the classical forms of capitalism it was much less successful in its ultimate conclusions concerning an early fall of the capitalist system. It was even less able to describe those socio-economic conditions determinative for a socialist solution.

The problem of the heterogeneous and ineffectual character of the laboring masses made it difficult from the beginning for proponents of socialism to place the working class within their theoretical schemes. For this reason we find in most of socialist theories, except for a few anarchistic inclinations, the disposition to accept the idea of state authority as a means of creating those circumstances propitious to the implementation of socialist ideas. It was previously shown that the idea of state authority, existent already in early utopian socialism, reached a central position in Leninist-Stalinist thinking as an instrument necessary to create not only an adequate social structure, but also to mold the still nonexistent communist man.

Although deemed necessary, the role of the state is loosely described by Marxism. This theory of the state itself is contradicted by another Marxian tenet, which predicted a gradual atrophy of the state after the takeover of power by the proletariat. In reality the state not only did not wither away but was continually reinforced. Furthermore, Marxism ascribed a great importance to the property structure as a basic condition for the emergence of the state. The idea that the state appeared only "where there is private property and a predatory class," proved to contain only limited historical truth and found limited proof in the workings of modern society. Actually, after the "socialist" revolution when the bureaucratic personnel by and large was changed and the structure of the leading class dramatically altered, the state and its coercive features remained intact and directed toward the same old social targets, the producers.

The other issue closely related to the theory of the state, the dictatorship of the proletariat, has not yet been elucidated enough. The Marxian prescriptions on this issue also were not confirmed by later historical developments. While it is true that the dictatorship of the proletariat managed to separate the old owners from their means of production it failed in other major assignments, namely, to create a socialist economy and a new type of citizen, the socialist man. Furthermore the elevation of proletarian elements to positions of leadership failed to give a proletarian profile to the dictatorship. It only managed to separate those elevated from their social roots, while the dictatorship itself became alienated from the toiling masses.

As early as the French Revolution, during the activity of its splinter Babouvist movement, it became at least partly clear that investing in an authoritative system was equal to accepting the possible permanence of that authority and the slight degree of equality obtained by such means was to be at the cost of freedom and individualism.

We have already seen that a distinctive place in the issues treated by Marxism is held by the theory of ownership of the means of production. Later, this issue was disputed by different strains of revisionism without being acceptably elucidated. The special emphasis of Marxism on the ownership aspects of social relations in defining social classes made it later difficult to explain the appearance of the new class of leaders whose historical role manifested itself precisely in its overwhelming control over the means of production without their property rights being clearly defined. Today, this nebulous juridical situation still exists and its solution appears to be dependent on the final shape of the economic format that the new class will take in its formative process. It is not yet totally clear whether property can be the sole determinant of the right to control the means of production or if there are other socio-economic and juridical factors which may complement, or even replace property rights. At the present time the new elite has been able to bypass the issue of property but we don't know for how long. There are some signs indicating that the accumulated wealth is so huge, and is increasing so rapidly, that its handling will make any type of property ownership, individual or limited collective, obsolete.

Another inadequately clarified issue of Marxism with serious consequences for the implementation of empirical socialism is the problem of social initiative. As we saw before, in the classical forms of the capitalist system initiative was motivated by self-interest, which constituted the elementary force for collective social achievements. Socialism did away with this factor for awhile while failing to replace it with an equally potent element. Self-interest became the focal point of communist policy when the system based on directives and coercion failed to yield the expected results. Up to this time the alternative environment prescribed by Marxism as a means of inhibiting the development of such egotistic attitudes as self-interest, failed to materialize. Again, one thing is certain. The fact that today communist countries have not been able to do away with individual egotism indicates the regimes' failure to create either a generating environment for the new type of man, or the collectivist individual of the future. What will from now on be the motivating force in communism is therefore as much a mystery as is communism itself.

A serious shortcoming of Marxist doctrine was its lack of emphasis on, and in time, on Lenin's part, the outright denial of the necessity of interweaving socialism with democracy. Marxism failed to indicate those socio-political factors which would have secured the survival and further development of liberal democracy in a socialist environment. Rejecting liberal bourgeois democracy meant the rejection of democracy in general. This helped bring to the surface those political-monopolistic tendencies in the Communist parties which separated the leaders from the party rank and file and promoted the physical and psychological separation of the party from the proletariat.

Despite their avowed commitment to proletarian hegemony, Marxism in general and Leninism in particular were skeptical of the proletariat's ability to lead the socialist revolution. One can find in the Marxian body of theory tangible elements which point to the fact that Marxism was ready to explain the onset of a socialist revolution not so much as the result of a conscious act of a matured proletariat, but as a direct result of the crisis of capitalism. In other words, if the crisis situation created a need for change even if the proletariat presumably did not exist, why was it necessary to imply that the change must occur for the benefit of the proletariat or, for that matter, that the change must be oriented toward socialism at all?

Previously we saw that by introducing the concept of proletarian dictatorship Marxism was able to delay the solution to the problem of the proletariat's lack of maturity without solving it in the end. Failure to solve this problem opened the door for the ascension to power of those revolutionary intellectuals who had the consciousness, willingness, aspiration and organizational ability to obtain the power. In consequence, after the conclusion of the revolutionary insurrection the proletariat found itself outside the realm of political power because of both its own lack of inertia and the unwillingness of the new political elite to share power with anyone. The myth of proletarian hegemony has continued, although by now it serves the sole purpose of legitimating an elite who actually entered into history proclaiming itself the redeemer of the toiling masses.

Despite their initial sincerity and dedication, the revolutionary intellectuals were unable to free the workers as a class. Instead, they opened the door to upward mobility for a chosen few. The revolutionary intellectuals were unable to fulfill their dream of being social liberators because their historical role was limited to the creation, by revolutionary means, of such politico-social conditions as were most conducive to rapid industrialization, and later, to the creation of an optimal milieu for the upcoming technological revolution.

Actually, no qualitative changes have occurred in the communist countries. All the steps taken in the name of socialism and presented as socialist achievements had already been implemented, on a bigger or smaller scale, in one capitalist country or another.

The revolutionary intelligentsia did not realize that their historical role was not a normative, morally justified action undertaken to achieve the much dreamed of social justice but, as later events confirmed, a historically brief and violent role for the prosaic purpose of creating a developed and centralized economy. They were not aware of the fact that their turn to go into oblivion would come soon, when their historic role and their social usefulness ended, and that their power would be challenged by another type of intellectual, the managerial technocrat.

A central issue connected with the social and economic situation of the toiling masses and extensively treated by Marxism is the issue of the alienation of the producers from the means of production and, in consequence, their alienation from the produced goods, and ultimately from the society in which they lived. Despite minute analysis of the problem, the final verdict of Marxist doctrine–that alienation in capitalist society is the direct consequence of the accumulation of the means of production in the form of private property–proved to be inadequate. First, the replacement of private property by state ownership did not solve the problem because state ownership fell short of socialization. In any case, socialization was impossible because of the inferior cultural-technical level of the masses. Second, the limited collective form of control over the means of production did not solve the problem either. Not only did the workers remain alienated but often segments of the new elite felt estranged from the reality in which they lived, and many of them still feel that their work does not serve the ideals for which they joined the movement. Thus, we still find alienation, not only among workers and those intellectuals who did not find their places in the system, but also those who reached important positions in the new hierarchy. This peculiar situation may be explained by the earliness of the phase in which the new class still evolves. The old property relations were destroyed while the new ones had no time to fully develop. The new elite imposed its control over the productive means but its ownership over them was not yet solved either formally or juridically.

If the Marxist doctrine failed to erect the theoretical structure of a socialist society and to give a clear picture of social, economic, political and moral relations which would typify a socialist society, the empirical experimentation of the Communist Parties with socialism was even less successful. All the measures taken by the Soviet Communist Party and other communist parties in power, were intended to solve some economic or political issues which were threatening with an imminent crisis. But the steps taken were far from being socialistic in nature and one cannot say that they were soluble only in a socialist context. In fact, any liberal West European party would have been able to do the same in a longer period. Any progressive party would have been able to industrialize, even with less sacrifices and brutality, and would have solved the agrarian problem, if not through collectivization but by means of capitalistic big agrarian enterprises. The end result would have been the same: concentration of both, industrial and agrarian capital for the sake of modernization.

The reality of fascism and of World War II, the destruction of European liberalism and the Soviet military occupation of Eastern Europe forced these countries to move in the direction of rapid transformation of their economy and society with a speed equal to a revolution.

In East European countries, there was a fortunate coming together, for the communist parties, between their ideological requirements and an objective necessity for the concentration of means of production and an increase in the state's role in the economy. This may explain the relative support given by the laboring masses at the beginning of the process when they indirectly profited from these transformations. Later, the same masses turned against the system when the collectivist measures started to work against them, when their interests and rights were encroached on and the contours of inequality and class privilege for the new elite took more definite forms. The alienation of the peasants was manifested more strikingly due to their resistance to any commonality, a sentiment they brought into cooperatives along with their most cherished lands.

The necessity for a speedy change in economic and social structures brought with it the necessity of adequate changes in social leadership, not only as a result of an inadequate development of the middle classes in Russia and Eastern Europe, but also as a legacy of the two world wars which had left these classes in disarray.

It is clear that a change in the social elite occurred in Russia and Eastern Europe after World War I and after World War II, but the true nature of these changes, their long term social and economic consequences, were not yet fathomed deeply enough to give a well-rounded theory of social evolution. Perhaps it is too early to offer some positive answers. It may be said though, that the social changes were more quantitative among the lower echelons and more qualitative among the higher echelons of society. In other words, the changes did run deeper among the social leadership, which underwent a complete change of guard, than among the common people whose number as a class increased while their social status and influence remained almost the same.

The obvious unfulfillment in the Soviet Union of the "socialist" goals or of what was thought to have a socialist essence, proded numerous scholars and activists of the socialist movement to account for the deviations and digressions from the Marxist platform. There were many interpretations and theories which appeared immediately after the first crises of the new system occurred. One of the first who tried to set up a systematic explanation was Trotsky. Despite his disillusionment with Soviet reality he still considered the Soviet experiment as a revolutionary process which had started with a socialist content but deviated from the egalitarian ideas because of the backwardness of the country and the bureaucratization of the party. Trotsky considered the deviation temporary, and the idea that Soviet reality, despite its collectivist forms, was not in its essence a socialist society, never crossed his mind.

Trotsky discounted the possibility that the "deviations" would be permanent, and the fact that the bureaucratized party apparatus was fulfilling a historical task along with a self-serving defense of its recently acquired privileges. What is important, though, is the fact that Trotsky had already recognized that in essence the deviation was a process of bureaucratization. Others, after Trotsky, emphasized this process perhaps too much, at the expense of a balanced theory.

The Italian author Bruno Rizzi, a leading member of the Italian Communist Party and a militant of the Fourth International, who finally transformed himself into an "independent socialist,"[1] is one of the prominent authorities who attempted to solve the Soviet puzzle. He tried to explain the phenomenon of unachieved social and economic domination by the workers using the theoretical instruments provided by Trotsky. Unsatisfied with these answers, however, he proceeded to develop his own theoretical version. In his opinion the Marxist prescription to concentrate all the means of production in the hands of the state and to suppress the market not only impedes the economic mechanism, but also leads to an overgrowth of the bureaucracy, which will tend to monopolize power and dominate the workers. For Rizzi bureaucratic domination represented a regression in history because the new class, due to its collective control over the means of production, became the owner of them. "Nationalization," declares Rizzi, "did not eliminate class property, it only made it collective,"[2] collective property of the bureaucracy. Thus, the type of social organization generated by expanding the state control over economic life presents all the characteristics of a class society: domination, oppression, exploitation, privileges.

On the same topic Luciano Pellicani confirms Karl Wittfogel's view that Marx let his revolutionary passion overcome his scientific reasoning when he consciously suppressed the economic-historic category of the Asiatic mode of production and continued to insist on the concentration of the means of production in the hands of the state. Despite the striking similarities between the functioning of the centralized and oppressive Asiatic mode of production and the type of socialism which Marxism envisaged; Marx continued to believe that state control would be an enormous step toward a superior form of freedom.

Later, Leszek Kolakowski, like many East European dissidents, confirmed the Rizzi theory of bureaucratization: "Nationalization and the authoritative planification make impossible an eventual development of a representative democracy," said Kolakowski.[3]

Rizzi does not give up the hope for socialism, but he wants a socialism based on the collective ownership by the workers over their enterprises and all the enterprises to be regulated by a market economy.

Inspired almost to excess by Rizzi's work was the well-known American scholar, James Burnham. His work *The Managerial Revolution* written in the early 1940s stirred the world of Marxian thinking with his far-reaching conclusions.

Burnham starts his argument by saying that in his lifetime "a period of rapid transition from one type of structure of society to another type"[4] is in process; that in this period the state, which even in the liberal era of the capitalist system was expected to have a limited role, that of securing the optimal conditions for an autonomous and private economy, is active in interfering in the economy by way of tariffs, subsidies, and the military stabilization of areas of potential capitalist investments. Today, state interference is obvious, open, and overwhelming. Such a statement leads one to the conclusion that an increase of such proportions of the socio-economic role of the state necessitates serious structural changes in economic and social life.

Burnham considers his theory as a third alternative, along with the two old ones, which either considered capitalism to be a permanent economic structure or one which would be replaced by socialism. His third alternative opted for a replacement of capitalist society by a "managerial society"[5] without pinpointing how capitalist or how socialist this managerial society would be. He explains the need for change by pointing to the inability of the contemporary capitalist system to handle its own resources, such as investments, technological development, market expansions, a growing public and private debt, etc. But Burnham rightly observes that a crisis which heralds the necessity for changes does not indicate that such a change must be of a socialist character. Although he criticized Marx for underestimating the life span allotted to capitalism[6] he agrees that capitalism had run its course and must be replaced by a managerial society. For Burnham, "Russia did not move toward socialism, at the same time did not move back to capitalism."[7] The Russian system, as he explains, is characterized by a drive for social dominance, for power and privilege, for the position of ruling class, by the social group of managers. It is based upon state ownership of the major instruments of production. "There will be no direct property rights in the major instruments of production vested in individuals as individuals."[8] Through this Burnham implies that property rights in the Soviet Union became superfluous and what counts is the state *apparat* which owns those means of production. But who are these managers? They are "certain individuals," explains Burnham, "the operating executives, production managers, plant superintendents, and their associates...those who organize the materials, tools, machines, plant facilities, equipment and labor...."[9] In other words, the future world belongs to the technocracy, both technical and administrative. But the intrinsic character of this society is not yet fully revealed, that is, whether it is exploitative or not or whether in its ultimate stage the system will return a part of the profit to the producers or not, although Burnham made a slight observation that the function of the managers is mainly to achieve profitability.[10]

The attitude of the capitalists toward state ownership and control of the economy is described by Burnham as hostile because, "like Leninists, they rightly sense that in the long run, if not at once, it is anticapitalist in its historical effects."[11] Burnham's interpretation is self-contradictory because it is historically demonstrated that private ownership is only a vehicle to secure the right of disposal over the means of production, and what actually motivated capitalism and created the phenomenon of alienation was precisely the right of disposal over the product of other's labor. The eradication of private ownership cannot imply the end of capitalism. Capitalism will survive, in modified form and with it will survive the sense of alienation.

Further on Burnham describes the managerial society as a totalitarian society because it has at its disposal modern technology, especially rapid communications and transportation, which allows the system to control every facet of public private life.[12] While this is partially true, one can go even further in stating that paternalism is an inevitable product of advanced technology, which requires such a system because of its dependence on large-scale promotion and development. There is, it seems, a dialectical reciprocity between technology and centralism. Each needs and presumes the existence of the other.

As to the question of who would rule the managerial society, the managers or the political bureaucrats, Burnham's answer is equivocal when he states that it is not important which group gains the upper hand as long as the system develops the required structural and institutional organization. In fact there is a tendency toward a fusion of the two groups due to the tendency of the managerial society to intermix politics and economics.[13] While this may be true in the long run, for the immediate future there have lately been signs that political bureaucrats often act against the managers in whom they see potential competitors in the power struggle and a threat to their acquired privileges. At the same time, managers see in some political bureaucrats dilettantes who know little or nothing about how to run the intricate components of the economy. There is a strong possibility in the near future of a show-down between managers and political bureaucrats rather than a coalescing process between the two.

In the light of the latest political events when many countries, mostly in Eastern Europe, have turned away from the methodology of centralization, and are embracing the ideals of democracy in politics and free enterprise in the economy, one may get the impression that the days of centralization are over. This is not so. The process of centralization of the economy is still in progress in the West. Although a hyper form of centralization had developed under Lenin and Stalin, it proved to be premature and exaggerated. A loose centralization, giving wide latitude to private entrepreneurship in economics and democracy in politics, under the protective umbrella of an enlightened state paternalism seems to be the form of the future society. This statement will appear logical considering that in a modern society individual needs are satisfied by social activity, and technological requirements are fulfilled by extensive scientific progress. All these activities require a great deal of investment and the mobilization of scientific forces made possible by economic concentration and the use of resources that can only be obtained through taxation.

Other theories that try to explain the deviation of empirical socialism from theoretical Marxism, such as Sweezy's and Battelheim's, interpret the period since the Russian Revolution of 1917 as a transition period, and see strong signs of a return to the capitalist system. In Sweezy's view the return is built into the system and is expressed by the autonomy of many enterprises and the increasing role of the market and material incentives as particular capitalist functions. This theory is rejected by Battelheim, who considers these factors to be secondary, the main reason for the return being not economic factors but political ones. The fact that "the proletariat has lost its power to a new bourgeoisie, with the result that the revisionist leadership of the Communist Party of the Soviet Union is today the instrument of this new bourgeoisie"[14] is the key to explaining today's Society society. Battelheim further argues that the return to the market and material incentives, and contradictions between planning and the market, are "surface effects" caused by deeper contradictions "situated at the level of the production relationships and productive forces."[15] Both positions actually fall short of historical reality. First, the market does not necessarily have to be capitalist; in fact it appeared well before capitalism and continued to exist continuously after the "socialist" revolution, albeit in restricted forms. Also, the "contradiction" between the market and planning are surface contradictions, and here Battelheim is right, the dominance of one over the other cannot be indicative and does not characterize the existing social system. Second, all these categories—market, planning, material incentives, the relative autonomy of enterprises, or submission to central directives–can empirically work for either system, capitalist or socialist.

On the other hand Battelheim falls short of reality when he states as a reason for the return of capitalism the loss of power on the part of the proletariat. Actually, the proletariat has never gained political power. What happened after the Russian Revolution of 1917 is that the appearance of proletarian power proved to be only an illusion amid the increasingly open assumption of power first by the political intellectuals (intellectual revolutionaries) and later increasingly by the administrative-technocrat intellectuals (intelligentsia).

Battelheim is right when he finds the essence of the contradictions at the production relations level. It is here that the character of a society is delineated. Control of the means of production, less the ownership relations and more the directive role played in production is the determinative element no matter whether the society is capitalist or socialist. What actually is important though is that the old dichotomous system survived the "socialist" revolution.

For Sweezy the process that has predominated in the Communist bloc is one of a return to capitalist methodology and this turn not only has directional consequences for policy but is having a serious impact on the class structure of the elite because of the ascent of a managerial bureaucracy. Further on it appears that both Sweezy and Battelheim leave the door open for a possible correctional intervention by the state in this process in order to reorient the direction of the development back to the socialist track. In Sweezy's case it would be by the suppression of capitalist economic methodologies, in Battelheim's case by giving a real meaning to the dictatorship of the proletariat by arming the masses with real political power.

Actually the danger of a return to capitalism does not exist. Such a return is not possible because the "socialist" revolution did not do away with capitalism in the first place. It is true that a serious modification occurred in the shift from private ownership to a limited collective ownership, and that the old bourgeois guard was replaced with a new bourgeoisie, but the exploitive relations survived together with the economic and political means to secure such exploitation. In other words, one cannot return to something that has never been abandoned. What is actually happening in some countries is a switch from a highly centralized to a less centralized economic methodology.

Sweezy's argument that the only way to return to the socialist path is through a repoliticization of Soviet society,[16] with a move toward mass initiative, toward a new cultural revolution or something even more drastic which would bring about a structural change in the new elite class, is only partially validated by history. The Chinese cultural revolution was unable to put the masses in charge of their political and economic destiny and similarly, the new democratized societies of Eastern Europe seem unable to go all the way in eradicating centralism and achieving a dominant role for the masses.

According to Sweezy, the historical factors responsible for the deviation from the presumed socialist direction were the impact of civil war and foreign intervention following the October Revolution which decimated the proletariat, rendering it unable to assume leadership and opening the way for other social strata to fill the political vacuum. This interpretation is typical of those offered by adherents of Marxist ideology who are frustrated by the consistent inapplicability of the major Marxian tenets concerning proletarian hegemony in the implementation of socialism. Their rigid adherence to the ideological prescriptions make it impossible for them to reevaluate social categories, in this case the politico-economic potentialities of the proletarian class. Consequently, they must explain the failure of the proletariat to assume the duties of leadership as a result of traumatic events such as war and revolution and not in terms of what the proletariat was actually able to do. But Sweezy is not consistent in his theory when later he recognizes that the "socialist man" in fact never appeared, while the "bourgeois man" was born and matured in a feudal world, and his economic activity acted through the centuries to mold his personality, conscience, and ideology. By the time the bourgeoisie was ready to take over the reins of society its character was fully formed. If one acknowledges, as Sweezy does, that the socialist man cannot be the result of a conscious and voluntarist act but emerges only after a long and tedious process of objective economic and ideological development,[17] then one cannot predict precisely which class will become the future hegemon. The theory of temporary stewardship by the revolutionary intellectuals, who presumably had to take on the role of hegemon till the political maturation of the proletariat, was refuted by history when the intellectual-revolutionaries became economic reformers instead of the cultural and political catalysts of the proletariat's evolution.

In the end Sweezy must conclude that

> ...the Russian experience...provides a devastating proof of the impossibility of infusing seemingly socialist forms–such as nationalized means of production and comprehensive economic planning–with genuine socialist content unless the process goes hand-in-hand with the formation of socialist human beings.[18]

There are similar conclusions in the works of dissenting East European authors such as Otta Sic, Rudolf Bahro, George Konrád and Iván Szelényi, to mention only a few.

Otta Sic considers the deviation from the socialist line a result of the bureaucratization of the system, a process imposed by an underdeveloped economy further ravaged by war and revolution and the lack of economic and technical experts. All these factors led to an antidemocratic solution of the social and economic problems, making the system's "one-man management" versus "collective management" a minor issue in comparison with the major dispute between the proponents of the leading role of the party and those who believed in self-government by the workers in a communist society.[19] The antidemocratic solutions extended the previous class relations by establishing a new dictatorship of a minority over the majority. This new dictatorship necessitates the creation of a larger bureaucracy to administer it, which in turn is concerned with "promoting special interests and possibly counteracting oppositional interests."[20]

The unprecedented expansion of the bureaucracy, explains Sic, was made possible by the elimination of the capitalist class to which it was previously subordinated. The process is continued by the concentration of power in the hands of a party-bureaucratic minority, whose particular interests become more and more visible and predominant.

Sic is mistaken when he considers the bureaucracy to be the consequence of negative historical factors and attributes to it a negative historical role. Actually, the growth of bureaucracy appears as a necessity and its rejection on the basis of its early inefficiency is wrong. Bureaucracy has not yet finished its social role. There are signs of increasing improvement with the advancement of technology and management systems which at the present time are undergoing a genuine revolution.

Sic's theory that a proper understanding of labor remuneration "not only on the basis of a mechanically measured quantity and quality of work, but also in view of the actual economic value produced for the benefit of society,"[21] would have helped to curtail the emergence of bureaucratic supremacy, is murky and not fully demonstrated. Theoretically it would be the role of the bureaucracy to ensure, in time, the production of such goods and services as society needs, through a scientific knowledge of such needs, and thereby to gradually eliminate the balancing role of the market which, despite its dynamism, is in essence wasteful. Only by fulfilling this role can the bureaucracy prove its economic and social indispensability, and therefore its historical justification.

Rudolf Bahro, a representative of East German dissent, acquired fame with the formulation of a new theoretical position that is equally critical of Eastern totalitarianism and Western capitalism, and offers a third way as an alternative to both capitalism and empirical socialism. Although Bahro's theory can be applied as a critique of both social systems it is not a theory of convergence, as Herbert Marcuse emphasized, but rather a formulation based on the similarities found in both systems.[22]

For Bahro the dissolution of private property did not resolve the main contradiction of the capitalist system, the social character of production and the private acquisition of the product. Bahro separates the fate of private property from the fate of human emancipation. For him "the increase in productivity and the abolition of private ownership of the means of production do not have to lead to socialism, they do not necessarily break the chains of domination, the subjugation of human beings to labor."[23] For Bahro the flow of events tends to stabilize and perpetuate the subjugation. First, it is justified by a lag in the economic, military, and technological competition with capitalism and later, when the new form of domination is established, its tenure becomes indefinite.[24] The way to break this vicious circle is through the intelligentsia, who integrate best into the elitist structure of society. This is because of the special place reserved for intellectuals in a society where knowledge and information are crucial to an economy based on advanced technology and science, and where the intellectuals share with the party functionaries the privileges, material benefits, and culture.[25] The new inequality between direct producers and intellectuals is expected to be dissipated through the advancement of technology which, by making the need for intellectual labor general, will make the intellectual character of the new type of producers universal. The only shortcoming in such a scenario seems to be its overoptimism. Unfortunately, historical evidence points to the fact that only a limited segment of the direct producers will become intellectual; the rest will become superfluous as their physical labor is replaced by rapidly advancing automation.

The absence of mass initiative forces Bahro to accept the temporary necessity of state, bureaucracy, and party. He suggests a way out in which socialism creates its own antistate and its own system of administration, with the gradual building up of self-management and cooperative systems.[26] The trouble with such a solution is that the achievement of such systems requires mass initiative, and so instead of providing an answer it only delays the solution. In fact, it brings back the whole Leninist scenario with its two-stage theory and delay of the withering away of the state until there occurs either the cultural and scientific rise of the proletariat or its demise and replacement by a universal intellectual.

An explanation similar to Bahro's is suggested by the Hungarian sociologists Konrád and Szelényi. For them the recurring cyclical crises of capitalism with all their negative effects, the need for massive and rapid investments in the development of the infrastructure, the increased arms race, the failure of traditional institutions like the church to organize education, necessitated increasing state intervention and supervision in both the East and the West, but more visibly in Eastern Europe. Consequently the continuous expansion of state bureaucracy, accompanied by a steady process of nationalization can be observed. In the swollen bureaucracy many intellectuals find an arena for their activity, especially because of the increasingly specialized technical requirements of the bureaucracy.[27] The modernizing role of the bureaucracy in Eastern Europe requires the ascension of the intellectuals to power. Due to the strong lingering presence of semifeudal relations in Eastern Europe, Konrád and Szelényi see the way to modernize as not through an eventual bourgeois revolution but through the workings of the bureaucratic state. For these authors, the Communist Party as the embodiment of the authority of the working class is a euphemism for the universalization of bureaucratic relations and for power in the hands of the intellectuals. They find similarities between the rational distributive system (i.e., socialism) and such redistributive systems like the Asiatic mode of production, where a centralized state bureaucracy plays a primary role. In such systems, the role played by the centralized bureaucratic apparatus in directing and organizing the social and economic activities, is the main avenue of legitimation in contrast with the modern redistributive economies (i.e., capitalism) where performance and dynamic growth are the primary means of legitimation.[28] This interpretation suggests that the bureaucratic system by its very format, is intrinsically lacking in dynamism.[29] In such a bureaucratic network concern for performance is replaced by a strict adherence to the bureaucratic ethos, team psychology, and subordination to the rules.

In the rational distribution system, according to Konrád and Szelényi, expert knowledge emerges as the dominant legitimizing principle, conferring for the first time on intellectuals the right of disposal over the surplus product and emancipating them from the social stratum they enjoyed during the classical period of capitalism, to a class position in which they can claim social hegemony in the postindustrial era.[30]

Konrád and Szelényi describe the natural resentment of the intellectuals toward the instability and irrationality of the market[31] as the basis for their efforts to develop a rational system of organizing the economy which in overall proportions and in the long run is superior to the market even though it often shows signs of rigidity and lack of dynamism. The new economic and political format, though, presents many other advantages, such as protecting the power structure from shifts in public opinion,[32] which often do harm in democratic systems by delaying the implementation of rational decisions.

In developing their theory, Konrád and Szelényi separate the intellectuals from the elite when they talk about Stalin's strivings to elevate the elite "above the intellectual class and above the party as a whole."[33] But they do not clarify the socioeconomic and political essence of the elite or the conflicts inside the intellectual group. For Konrád and Szelényi the following is absolutely clear though:

> Not every party member belongs to the ruling elite; not even every intellectual who belongs to the party can belong to the elite. But it is clear that no one can be a member of the elite who is not both party member and an intellectual.[34]

BALANCE SHEET AND CONCLUSIONS

In conclusion it may be said that socialist theory, both in its classical Marxist forms and in its revisionist variants, failed to provide a well rounded formula for achieving socialism and the little that was provided did not match historical reality. In response to this deficiency, as has been partially shown above, came a wealth of theories which ascribed the empirical forms of socialism in the Soviet Union and its East European counterparts, to the bureaucratization of the system. This bureaucratization was caused either by political deviation from the socialist line, or was the inevitable product of an overgrown state apparatus necessitated by the requirements of industrialization and modernization. For some authors this deviation is only temporary, for others it is the end result of the "socialist" revolution, a system which is here to stay and for whose full development only time is needed. While some authors speak about a bureaucratic class in general, others differentiate among the state bureaucracy, the economic-administrative bureaucracy, and managers. Others see in the growth of the bureaucracy a way for the intellectuals to achieve power as a new dominant class despite its internal differences and conflicts. For some analysts the deviations are describing a large circle back to capitalism, for others they are taking society to a new social formation whose features remain as nebulous as that of socialism itself.

At this moment one must raise the question of what actually happened in Eastern Europe and Russia, and what caused the deviations from the logic of the Marxist line? Let us answer the second question first. Recapitulating the causes of deviation, one finds the following:

1. Marxism, though it achieved remarkable success in analyzing the capitalist mode of production, failed to draw the right

conclusions concerning the life span of the capitalist system (and thus erroneously predicting the imminence of socialism), and wrongly attributed to the proletariat hegemonical characteristics which it never had and never actually developed. These two major miscalculations produced serious distortions in other, less significant hypotheses, leaving the whole doctrine with few applicable prescriptions.

2.   Marxism was permeated with too many normative elements relating to abstract justice and with too much revolutionary passion to produce an objective, scientific prognosis of the economic and social development of the twentieth century. Consequently there is a wide gap between the doctrine and historical reality.

3.   The revisionist attempts to lessen the gap between Marxism and reality were too political, being motivated either to refute or to defend Marxism. The authors of these revisionist attempts were too entrenched within the Marxian framework of thinking, and tried to revise Marxism without relinquishing their commitment to the major Marxian tenets and dictums.

4.   The willingness of the proletariat to build a socialist society was overestimated. Being products of the capitalist system, the industrial proletariat saw it as natural to sell their labor for wages. Their only real concern was for the equitability of those wages, not their eradication. After the "socialist" revolution there were only slight grumblings over the disposition of political power and much more over the value of the wages. The proletariat in the "new historical era" remained wage earners, as they had been under classical capitalism. As a rule the proletariat exhibits the moral characteristic of capitalism, the pursuit of self-interest. Destroying this feature would mean the elimination of a way of thinking which comes natural to all classes produced by capitalism.

The worker's interest was limited to the material conditions of his person and his immediate family, his wages, working conditions, and job security. His interests in communal affairs were limited to economic betterment and limited cultural intercourse. His interest in politics was kindled only to the extent to which the general interest overlapped his own individual interest. His individualism was molded by its creator, capitalism, and his sense of "collectivism" existed only marginally. He became revolutionary not by instinct or because of the social position of his class, but when the business of capitalism went wrong and was unable to provide the minimal requirements the workers were used to, and they were unable to secure the basic livelihood created under conditions of normal economic growth.

5. Marxism was mistaken in believing that the workers were interested in the eradication of private ownership as earlier the bourgeoisie were interested in expanding their commercial-industrial activities and in eliminating all the obstacles hindering such activities. Unlike capitalism, which opposed everything representing feudalism, the proletariat was created by capitalism, and its existence was justified by capitalism. It may be said that while the bourgeoisie became capitalist by practicing capitalism the workers' activity under socialism ended in a dead end street because it continued in its basic role, that of alienated creator of surplus value.

6. Marxism had put too much emphasis on private property as generator of the class system and the state. The dissolution of private property did not alleviate the dichotomous nature of society. It changed only its external forms.

7. The historical role of the dictatorship of the proletariat has been mythified and its impact on society and the economy exaggerated. While the communist dictatorship was able to bring about some economic and social dislocations its impact was confined to the perimeters of capitalist methodology. The dictatorship of the proletariat did not secure workers' rule and even less was it able to create the new socialist man.

8. Marxism overestimated the impact of mass initiative. When, after the revolution it failed to justify itself, the regime was compelled to return to the old methodology based on self-interest and individual initiative.

9. Empirical socialism was never able to fulfill the Marxist promises of a socialist-democratic society. In order to implement what was believed to be socialist relations the regime found

it increasingly necessary to develop totalitarian methods, thus exposing the unpopular nature of these relations. The masses remained alienated, both from empirical socialism which was too oppressive, and from Marxist ideology, which was too complex for them to understand and too utopian to be implemented.

10. Marxism overemphasized the reform potential of the class struggle and revolution. One of the basic tenets of Marxism is the idea that class struggle is the driving force in history and, together with revolution, will redress the social injustices generated by an unfair mode of production. In reality, though, the true driving and creative force in society proved to be the individual's ambition to achieve success over other competing individuals. The actual role of the class struggle was a destructive one, namely to annihilate those conditions which were propitious for the ambition to achieve individual success without the guarantee that the motivations that replaced the pursuit of profit would be morally more justified or lead to a more successful society.

Returning to the first question, that of the nature of the changes in Eastern Europe and Russia, it is imperative to clarify whether the new system is socialist or capitalist. A third alternative, exhibiting totally different characteristic of class relations toward the means of production, would be unlikely. Theoretically, a system must either be based on the equality of classes or the subordination of one class by another. Even if a system combines both socialistic and capitalistic elements, one or the other must prevail and the society must exhibit a leaning either toward capitalism or toward socialism; an ambiguous *status quo* can only be of a transient nature. It is the economic and social, and from there the political, relations of the classes toward each other, and each separately toward the means of production, which determines the profile of a society. If the prevailing conditions are that of subordination of the lower class with initiative coming from the upper levels of the society, and if an elite administers the social product and determines the quantity of surplus product to be returned to the producers, then we are dealing with a capitalist formation whatever the external forms of that formation may be.

Historically it has been proven that capitalism can appear in different forms according to the developmental level and nature of the means of production. In its very early stages, in the fourteenth and fifteenth centuries, when typical capitalist methods were restricted to money accumulation, capitalism appeared in the form of banking. Later, when the transactions went beyond the monetary systems and included an ever growing exchange of goods, capitalism acquired a commercial character. And even later, when more and more capital was invested in manufacturing and development of productive resources, capitalism entered in the industrial stage of its development. In the late nineteenth and early twentieth centuries capitalist enterprise became more concentrated and capital became universal, merging commercial, banking, and industrial activities in huge conglomerates overlapping geographic borders of the capitalist countries. It was the monopolistic stage of capitalism. This stage continues today, along with signs that capitalism is changing its form again, entering in a super technological age in which capital concentration will reach its climax. What the Soviet bloc has experienced since the Bolshevik Revolution is a new form of capitalism geared to the management of a super-concentrated economy, the handling of a technological revolution, and unprecedented investments in manufacturing. All the talk about the implementation of socialism proved to be a myth, exploded by the reality of capitalist relations surviving, in a modified form, the "Socialist revolution."

The history of recent capitalist developments has proved that the concentration of capital can be achieved in two different ways according to the development level of the means of production, political traditions (democratic or totalitarian), and historical circumstances (traumas of wars fought on national soil and revolutions). Thus, in this century the same process was achieved through two different methodologies: In the East by extra-economic, brutal and coercive means (revolution, nationalization), in the West through competition and economic expansion that involves incorporating the assets of those proven weaker in the competitive process. Either process though, leads toward economic uniformity, technical standardization, centralization and concentration of the economy, social regimentation, which took the form of (communism in the East, and fascism in the West), and increased state interference and control. The similarity of aims on the part of both economic processes was precisely the reason many parallels have been drawn between the two systems and why the theory of convergence between capitalism and "socialism" has been advanced.

A significant difference between the two methodologies can be observed on the social and political levels. While capitalist countries maintained, by and large, their democratic-parliamentary systems and a dichotomous social structure, consisting of entrepreneurs and executors, the "socialist" countries, while maintaining the same dichotomous structure, made significant qualitative changes among the entrepreneurs and quantitative changes among the executors. Socially, the "socialist" countries established a hierarchy that included not only the subservient classes but also the elite. A new type of quasi-feudal system is recreated in this new type of capitalism with a well defined and institutionalized hierarchy of position and rank, and imposing reciprocal obligations on citizens toward one another and toward the state. It is a hierarchy with its own Marxist ideology (formally acknowledged but little implemented) and its particular ethos. Oddly enough, this system, antidemocratic to its core, was built on the principles of democratic centralism developed by Lenin, which in its theoretical form was meant to secure the political supremacy of the rank and file in the party and among the masses in society. In this system the production arrangements of free enterprise are replaced by a system which appears awkward, uneconomic and bureaucratic, and through which antiquated forms of human relations are resuscitated. Conservatism replaces innovation; rigid, simplistic norms replace variation and creativity, and solutions appropriate to the complexity of the modern world are stifled; dogmas replace free thinking. In this system loyalty must be directed toward the "masses," embodied in the political institutions of the "dictatorship of the proletariat": party and state.

Functionally, this system involves a modern version of the Asiatic mode of production, with a feudalistic type of social pyramid of interlocking relations from superior to inferior. Here there is a well-defined collective and individual responsibility toward the state for both the social leaders in their reciprocal relations, and the masses in their subordination to this new type of suzerainty.

The reality of this theory is confirmed by the historical process itself. In the history of civilization, regardless of the mode of production, two basic types of development can be discerned: slow and explosive. The eras of slow development, the Asiatic mode of production, and the feudal, had a relatively longer span of evolution characterized by a slow quantitative aggrandizement of material goods and relatively slow improvement of the already discovered technological and cultural achievements. The explosive eras, certain periods of antiquity, the middle ages, and the age of capitalism, are shorter, and display a rapid development in the production of material goods, new discoveries, and fascinating cultural achievements. These are the eras in which human creativeness reaches its culmination. It seems, though, that the slowly developing systems, while appearing incongruous and awkward, are necessary stages in the process of human development, which consists of alternating explosive dynamism and slow and steady growth. It can be observed that the slow-evolving eras are characterized by a well defined social organization with little social mobility, with deeply rooted habits and traditions in which each individual finds his established role in the complicated social mechanism. Individuals enjoy social protection and security but there is little room for growth beyond the limits already established by the existing social laws. In the explosive eras the social norms are more loosely defined, with a free, up or down, social mobility; with little security but with a lot of room for achievement and creativity. These are the eras of great scientific and technological discoveries, and also the eras of social innovation and transformation.

It seems that capitalism, like antiquity and the middle ages, undergoes both dynamic and slow-moving change. Perhaps the changes in social and economic structure, which were more noticeable in the Soviet bloc and less evident in the West, are accommodations of capitalism to its new stage. The high level of capital concentration slowly removes competition and with it the element of dynamism, but it also removes the insecurities of the marketplace. It seems that the end process of capital concentration will be the establishment of a more stable economic system with vast resources of investment needed for the greatly increased technological requirements of the twenty-first century.

As was mentioned before, the economic changes that took place in Eastern Europe under communism had a direct impact on the social structure, changing mainly the class content of the elite and introducing a high level of bureaucratization. The theories explaining the nature of the new social leadership, as already seen, are numerous and often contradictory, but in most cases they convey a grain of truth. First, it can be said that the "socialist" elite is better organized and more bureaucratized than any previous bureaucracies. Second, the bureaucratic system which envelopes the whole society with a web of organizations does not represent a monolithic unity. It is broken by interest groups along the vertical line of organization. Third, political power is not vested in the bureaucracy as a whole but is concentrated in the higher echelons of the party and the state. Fourth, the new elite came to power mainly due to the impotence of the previous middle classes to meet the economic exigencies of post industrialization. It came to power as the representative of the working masses, a belief sanctioned by its Marxist ideology which also gave it legitimation as social organizer. Fifth, the Marxist doctrine, due to its shortcomings, became less and less usable as a theory of social organization. Those new forms of collectivity introduced were done not to achieve a socialistic goal but to mobilize the masses for an extensive economic reconstruction and sacrifices, and also to enable the leadership to control and manage the growing economy, which became more complex and sophisticated. Sixth, the complexity of the economy and of technology required a much greater role for the intellectual in the social organization. We are witnessing an intellectualization of the bureaucracy. But the class interests of the intellectuals are not uniform. There are many intellectuals, in fact the majority, who have no share in the political power. Historically the role of the intellectuals has been limited to the function of culture generator and class servant. In the new situation, their importance is enhanced, although only a few of them are directly in a position of social hegemony. Seventh, the heterogenous content of the intellectual strata and their differentiated roles in the social hierarchy make it vulnerable to internal political competition. At the present time the old intellectual group in power, the revolutionary intellectuals, mainly ideologues, activists, and journalists, are becoming more and more intensively pressured by a new group of intellectuals, the technocratic-administrative managers. There is a possibility that in the near future there will be a showdown between these two segments of the same social stratum. This conflict seems to boil down to a matter of what social function will be performed in time by which group of intellectuals. If the function of the political bureaucracy, as suggested by Burnham, was that of midwife for the new era, separating the capitalist from his ownership,[1] then the function of the managerial segment of the intellectuals is to organize and to bring the economy to its highest degree of concentration.

Therefore it can be said that capital concentration and the new organization of productive forces can be the real revolution, perhaps even greater than the technological-scientific revolution, holding an immeasurable potential for smooth and balanced growth. At the same time, technical development and automation may have its negative side, from the economic point of view, by transforming a good part of the labor force into a superfluous mass of unneeded population, a situation similar to that of the English nation during the period of land enclosures from the late fifteenth to the early nineteenth centuries.

In consequence, one may argue that the system of concentration and centralization is here to stay despite temporary efforts at decentralization and periodical returns to the methodology of classical capitalism, as happened during the 1960s and later. These measures were only temporary solutions for deficiencies and lack of experience in running the new economy.

A centralized and totally planned economy will be possible and desirable only when human civilization knows the hidden forces that move the economic process and drive technological progress. Until then the market cannot be disregarded. In fact it has never been completely abolished, it remains the main avenue toward economic concentration, which is a product of competitive economic successes and failures.

NOTES

Notes to Foreword

1.   Leszek Kolakowski, *Main Currents of Marxism* (Oxford: Clarendon Press, 1978), Vol. II, p. 350.

2.   V. I. Lenin, "What Is To Be Done?" *Selected Works* (Moscow: Progress Publishers, 1967), Vol. I, pp. 118, 122.

3.   See the chapter, "The Dialectic of the Soviet State," in Herbert Marcuse, *Soviet Marxism* (New York: Columbia University Press, 1958).

4.   Peter Dodge, ed. *A Documentary Study of Hendrick de Man, Socialist Critic of Marxism.* (Princeton: Princeton University Press, 1979), pp. 313-314.

5.   Milovan Djilas, *The Unperfect Society, Beyond the New Class* (New York: Harcourt, Brace & World Inc., 1969), p. 18. This work is a continuation of his first book *The New Class,* published much earlier in 1957, in which he departs from his communist position.

Notes to Chapter I

1.   Kolakowski, L. *Main Currents of Marxism.* (Oxford: Clarendon Press, 1978), I, 184.

See also Wilhelm Weitling, *Garantien der Harmonie und Freiheit* (Berlin: Buchhandlung Borwnolte, 1908).

2.   Ibid., I, 88.

3.   Ibid., I, 190.

4.   Ibid., I, 208.

5.   Ibid., I, 216. See also Louis Blanc. *La Socialisme Droit au travail* (Paris: 1948) and *Discours Politiques* (Paris: Librairie Germer Baillire et cie, 1882), pp. 352-373.

6.   Ibid., I, 186.

7.   George Lichtheim, *The Origins of Socialism*, p. 194.

8.   Karl Marx and Frederick Engels, "Manifesto of the Communist Party" in *Selected Works* (Moscow: Foreign Languages Publishing House, 1962), pp. 36, 37, 38.

9.   Lichtheim, *The Origins of Socialism*, p. 206.

10.   Ibid.

11.   Marx and Engels, "Manifesto," in *Selected Works* (Moscow: Foreign Languages Publishing House, 1962), I, 40.

12.   Ibid., I, 41.

13.   Ibid., I, 43.

14.   Ibid., I, 46.

15.   Ibid., I, 43.

16.   Ibid., I, 41.

17.   Leszek Kolakowski, *Main Currents of Marxism*, I, 359.

18.   M. M. Bober, *Marx's Interpretation of History* (New York: W. W. Norton, 1965), p. 272.

19.   Henry Chambre, *From Karl Marx to Mao Tse-Tung* (New York: P. J. Kennedy and Sons, 1959), p. 182.

20.   M. M. Bober, *Marx's Interpretation of History*, p. 273.

21.   Ibid., p. 275. See also Marx "Critique of the Gotha Programme" in Karl Marx and Frederick Engels, *Selected Works* (Moscow: Foreign Languages Publishing House, 1962), pp. 13-48.

22.   Ibid., p. 277. See also F. Engels, *Anti-Dühring* (New York: International Publishers, 1939), pp. 125, 310, and F. Engels, "Socialism, Utopian and Scientific" in *Selected Works* (Moscow: Foreign Languages Publishing House, 1962), Vol. II, pp. 116-156.

23.   Leszek Kolakowski, *Main Currents of Marxism*, vol. I, p. 131.

24.   M. M. Bober, *Karl Marx's Interpretation of History*, p. 258.

25.   Ibid., p. 259, see also Karl Marx, *Capital*, vol. III, pp. 304, 522. In this work Marx tries to analyze in detail the economic mechanism of the capitalist system from which he arrives at his final conclusion on the necessity to replace capitalism with socialism.

26.   Ibid., p. 260. See also Karl Marx, *Capital*, vol. III, pp. 516-517.

Notes to Chapter II

1.   *Leninism and the World Revolutionary Working Class Movement* (Moscow: Progress Publishers, 1976), pp. 330-31.

2.   Ibid.

3.   Lenin, V. I., *The Dictatorship of the Proletariat and the Elections to the Constituent Assembly* (New York: Contemporary Publishers Association, 1920), p. 20.

4.   Lenin, V. I., "What is to be done?" *Selected Works*, Vol. I, p. 122; also Lenin, V. I., *Collected Works* (Moscow: Foreign Languages Publishing House, 1960), Vol. V, p. 386.

5.   Kolakowski, L., *Main Currents of Marxism,* Vol. I, p. 418.

6.   Lenin, V. I., *Collected Works,* Vol. 26, p. 94.

7.   Ibid.

8.   Lenin, V. I., "Imperialism the Highest Stage of Capitalism" *Selected Works* (Moscow: Progress Publishers, 1967), Vol. I, chap. I. (This work cannot be truly considered objective since it was written during World War I and analyzes capitalism in its cataclysmic period. Actually, capitalism proved much more resilient and able to reestablish itself after several similar crises in the future.)

9.   Known better under its more popular title "The April Thesis."

10.   Lenin, V. I., *Selected Works* (Moscow: Progress Publishers, 1967), Vol. I, pp. 772-773.

11.   Lenin, V. I. "Imperialism, the Highest Stage of Capitalism," in *Selected Works* (Moscow: Progress Publishers, 1967), Vol. I, 697-777.

Notes to Chapter III

1.   Lenin, V. I., *Selected Works,* (Moscow: Progress Publishers, 1967), Vol. I, p. 563.

2.   Lenin, V. I., *Collected Works* (Moscow: Foreign Languages Publishing House, 1962), Vol. 8, p. 297.

3.   Lenin, V. I., "Economics and Politics in the Era of the Dictatorship of the Proletariat," *Selected Works* (Moscow: Progress Publishers, 1967), Vol. 3, p. 275.

4.   Lenin, V. I., *The Dictatorship of the Proletariat and the Elections to*

the Constituent Assembly (New York: Contemporary Publishers Association, 1920), p. 16.

5.   Lenin, V. I., *The Dictatorship of the Proletariat and the Elections to the Constituent Assembly*, p. 18.

6.   Ibid., p. 22.

7.   Lenin, V. I., "Two Tactics of Social-Democracy in the Democratic Revolution," *Selected Works*, Vol. I, p. 561.

8.   Lenin, V. I., "First Congress of the Communist International," *Selected Works*, Vol. 3, p. 135.

9.   Lenin, V. I., "The Dictatorship of the Proletariat and Elections to the Constituent Assembly," p. 27.

10.   Lenin, V. I., "Two Tactics of Social-Democracy in the Democratic Revolution," *Selected Works*, (Moscow: Progress Publishers, 1967), Vol. I, p. 511.

11.   Lenin, V. I., "First Congress of the Communist International," March 2-6, 1919, *Selected Works* (Moscow: Progress Publishers, 1967), Vol. III, p. 134.

12.   Lenin, V. I., *Collected Works*, Vol. 31, p. 58.

Notes to Chapter IV

1.   Robert V. Daniels, *The Nature of Communism* (New York: Random House, 1962), p. 20.

2.   Ibid., p. 20.

3.   J. V. Stalin, "The Socialist Drive," *The Stalin Revolution* (ed. Robert V. Daniels, Boston: D. C. Heath and Company, 1965), p. 27; from J. V. Stalin "A Year of Great Change" ("On the Occasion of Twelfth Anniversary of the October Revolution" and "Problems of Agrarian Policy in the USSR"), speech delivered at the conference of Marxist students of the Agrarian Question, December 27, 1929.

4.   Leon Trotsky, "Soviet Bonapartism" in *The Stalin Revolution* (ed. Robert V. Daniels, Boston: D. C. Heath and Company, 1965), p. 98, from Leon Trotsky's *The Revolution Betrayed: What is the Soviet Union and Where is it Going?*

5.   Ibid., p. 100.

6.   Ibid.

7.   Ibid., p. 101.

8.   Ibid.

9.   Ibid., p. 103.

10.   Herbert Marcuse, *Soviet Marxism* (New York: Columbia University Press, 1958), p. 74.

11.   Ibid., p. 1.

12.   Ibid., p. 5.

13.   Ibid., p. 8.

14.   Ibid., p. 9.

15.   Ibid., p. 12.

16.   Ibid., p. 40.

17.   Ibid., p. 94.

18.   J. V. Stalin, *Political Report to the Sixteenth Party Congress* (New York: Workers Library Publishers, 1930), p. 171.

19.   Marcuse, *Soviet Marxism,* p. 104.

20.   Ibid., pp. 104-105.

21.   Ibid., p. 105.

22.   Ibid., p. 145.

23.   Ibid., p. 138.

24.   Ibid., p. 137.

25.   Raymond A. Bauer, "Ideological Revision," *The Stalin Revolution,* Robert V. Daniels, ed. (Boston: D. C. Heath and Co., 1965), p. 22.

26.   Ibid., p. 24.

27.   See Robert V. Daniels, *The Nature of Communism* (New York: Random House, 1962), p. 30.

28.   Ibid., p. 31.

29.   Ibid., p. 32.

30.   Ibid., pp. 31-32.

31.   Ibid., p. 34.

32.   Leon Trotsky, "Soviet Bonapartism," *The Stalin Revolution* (Robert V. Daniels, ed. 1965), p. 98 from Leon Trotsky's book *The Revolution Betrayed: What is the Soviet Union and Where is it Going?* (Garden City, N.Y.: Doubleday, Doran and Co., 1937).

33.   Robert V. Daniels, *The Nature of Communism,* p. 246.

Notes to Chapter V

1.   Alexander Erlich, "The Problem of Industrial Development," *The Stalin Revolution*, 1965, p. 7.

2.   Robert V. Daniels, *The Conscience of the Revolution*, pp. 51-52.

3.   Ibid., p. 81.

4.   Ibid.

5.   Ibid., pp. 82-83.

6.   Ibid., p. 83.

7.   Ibid., p. 120.

8.   Ibid., p. 121, quotation taken from Trotsky's "Dictatorship vs Democracy," p. 14.

9.   Ibid., p. 121, quotation taken from Trotsky's "Tezisy Tsk-RKP po trudu" (Theses of the CC of the RCP on Labor), Pravda, January 22, 1920.

10.   Ibid., p. 126.

11.   Ibid., p. 127.

12.   Ibid.

13.   Ibid., p. 128, quotations taken from "Workers' Opposition Theses on the Trade Unions," January 18, 1921, Vsesoyuznaya Kommunisticheskaya Partiya (bolshevikov) V rezoliutsiyakh Sezdov, Konferentsi i plenumov Tsk (The All-Union Communist Party [Bolshevik] in Resolutions and Decisions of the Congresses, Conferences, and Plenums of the Central Committee (Moscow, 1931), I, appendix, 813.

14.   Ibid., p. 128, quotation taken from Alexandra Kollontai, "The Workers' Opposition" (Chicago, 1921), p. 5.

15.   Ibid., p. 133.

16.   Ibid., p. 125.

17.   Ibid., p. 126, quotation taken from Lenin's "To the Organizations of the RCP (b), on the question of the Agenda of the Party Congress," March 2, 1920.

18.   Ibid., p. 135.

19.   Ibid., p. 137.

20.   Ibid., p. 143.

21.   Ibid., p. 144.

22.   Ibid., p. 144. See also Daniels' reference to the subject: Izvestiya Vremennogo Revoliutsionnogo Komiteta (News of the Temporary Revolu-

tionary Committee), appendix to Pravda O Kronshtadte (The Truth about Kronstadt, Prague, 1921).

23.   Manya Gordon, *The Stalin Revolution,* ed. 1965.

24.   Ibid., p. 33.

Notes to Chapter VI

1.   Moshe Lewin, "Collectivization: The Reasons," *The Stalin Revolution,* 1972, p. 76 from his article "The Immediate Background of Soviet Collectivization," *Soviet Studies* 17 (October 1965).

2.   Ibid., p. 79.

3.   Ibid., p. 82.

4.   Ibid., p. 85.

5.   Ibid., pp. 109-110, David J. Dallin, "The Return of Inequality."

6.   Ibid., p. 110.

Notes to Chapter VII

1.   Robert Daniels, *The Nature of Communism,* (New York: Random House, 1962), p. 107.

2.   Ibid.

3.   Barrington Moore, "The Renovation of Bureaucracy," *The Stalin Revolution* (1965), p. 52.

4.   Ibid., pp. 94-97, Rudolph Hilferding, "The Logic of Totalitarianism" from his book, *State Capitalism or Totalitarian State Economy* (1947).

5.   Ibid., p. 97.

6.   Ibid., pp. 95-96.

7.   Herbert Marcuse, *Soviet Marxism,* p. 105.

8.   Ibid.

9.   Ibid.

10.   Ibid.

11.   Ibid.

12.   Ibid., p. 109.

13.   Ibid., p. 110.

14.   Barrington Moore, "The Renovation of Bureaucracy," in *The Stalin Revolution,* pp. 52-53 from his article "Soviet Politics–the Dilemma of

Power: The Role of Ideas in Social Change" (Cambridge, Mass.: Harvard University Press, 1950), (Russian Research Center Studies No. 2).

15.   Ibid., p. 54.
16.   Ibid.

Notes to Chapter VIII

1.   Herbert Marcuse, *Soviet Marxism,* p. 111.
2.   Ibid., p. 111.
3.   Ibid., p. 112.
4.   Isaac Deutscher, *The Stalin Revolution* (ed. 1965), pp. 1-2.
5.   Robert V. Daniels, "The Struggle with the Right Opposition," *The Stalin Revolution,* (ed. 1965), pp. 13-15, 20 from his book "The Conscience of the Revolution: Communist Opposition in Soviet Russia" (Cambridge, Mass.: Harvard University Press, 1965). See also Trotsky's book "The Revolution Betrayed: What is the Soviet Union and Where is it Going?" (Doubleday, Doran and Co., 1937).
6.   Ibid., p. 214, Roy Medvedev, "The Social Basis of Stalinism," from his book *Let History Judge* (New York: Alfred A. Knopf, 1971).
7.   Ibid., pp. 217-229.

Notes to Chapter IX

1.   Bruno Rizzi, *Il Collettivismo Burocratico,* (Milano: SugarCo Sedizioni, 1977). See the introduction by Luciano Pellicani, p. 12.
2.   Bruno Rizzi, *Il Collettivismo Burocratico,* (Milano: SugarCo Sedizioni, 1977), p. 14.
3.   Leszek Kolakowski, *Main Currents of Marxism.* (Oxford: Clarendon Press, 1978), vol. III.
4.   James Burnham, *The Managerial Revolution* (New York: John Day Company, 1941), p. 9.
5.   Ibid., p. 29.
6.   James Burnham, *The Managerial Revolution,* (New York: John Day Company, 1941), p. 40.
7.   Ibid., p. 48.
8.   Ibid., pp. 71-72.
9.   Ibid., p. 82.

10.   Ibid., p. 83.

11.   Ibid., p. 114.

12.   Ibid., p. 152.

13.   Ibid., pp. 156-157.

14.   Paul M. Sweezy and Charles Battelheim, *On the Transition to Socialism* (New York and London: Monthly Review Press, 1971), p. 16.

15.   Ibid., pp. 18-19.

16.   Ibid., p. 84.

17.   Ibid., p. 111.

18.   Ibid., p. 118.

19.   Otta Sic, *The Communist Power System* (New York: Praeger Publishers, 1981), p. 17.

20.   Ibid., p. 55.

21.   Ibid., pp. 70-71.

22.   Ulf Wolter, ed., *Rudolf Bahro, Critical Responses* (White Plains, New York: M. E. Sharpe Inc., 1980), p. 25.

23.   Ibid., p. 28. See Herbert Marcuse, "Protosocialism and Late Capitalism: Toward a Theoretical Synthesis Based on Bahro's Analysis."

24.   Ibid., p. 28.

25.   Ibid., p. 29.

26.   Ibid., pp. 30-31.

27.   George Konrád and Iván Szelényi, *The Intellectuals on the Road to Class Power* (New York and London: Harcourt Brace Jovanovich, 1979), p. 128.

28.   Ibid., p. 50.

29.   Ibid., p. 170.

30.   Ibid., p. 63.

31.   Ibid., p. 70.

32.   Ibid., p. 170.

33.   Ibid., pp. 184-185.

34.   Ibid., p. 191.

Notes to Balance Sheet and Conclusions

1.   James Burnham, *The Managerial Revolution,* pp. 150-160.

WORKS CITED

Gazdaság (Economy). From 1969 through 1983.

I. ARTICLES

Bolland, Stefan. "Freedom of Decision Within the Framework of the Central Plan," Eastern European Economics, XI (1), Fall, 1972.

Bonifert, Donát. "'Piaci szocializmus' vagy tervszerü gazdaságirányitás?" ['Market Socialism' or Planned Economy?], *Közgazdasági szemle*, XXIII (6), June, 1976.

Göncö, György. "Az értéktörvény a kapitalizmusban és a szocializmusban" [The Law of Value in Capitalism and in Socialism], *Közgazdasági szemle*, V (5), May, 1958.

Halasi, László, "Árutermelés és munkaerö a szocializmusban" [Commodity Production and Labor in Socialism], *Közgazdasági szemle*, VIII (3), March, 1961.

Hegedüs, András, "Lenin és a szocializmus gazdálkodási rendszerének alternatívái" [Lenin and the Management Alternatives of Socialism], *Kö zgazdasági szemle*, XVII (4), April, 1970.

Mihálik, István. "Lenin az áru- és pénzviszonyok felhasználásáról a szocializmusban" [Lenin on the Employment of Commodity and Financial Relations in Socialism], *Társadalmi szemle*, XXV (3), March 1970.

II. BOOKS AND PAMPHLETS

Bahro, Rudolf, *The Alternative in Eastern Europe*. Norfolk: NLB, 1978.

Brzezinski, Zbigniew K. *The Soviet Bloc. Unity and Conflict*. Cambridge, Massachusetts: Harvard University Press, 1960.

Burnham, James. *The Managerial Revolution*. New York: The John Day Company, Inc., 1941.

Burnham, John. *Total War. The Economic Theory of a War Economy.* Boston: Meadow Publishing Company, 1943.

Chambre, Henri S. J., *From Karl Marx to Mao Tse-Tung. A Systematic Survey of Marxism-Leninism.* New York: P. J. Kennedy & Sons, 1963.

Dallin, Alexander, ed. *Diversity in International Communism.* New York & London: Columbia University Press, 1963.

Daniels, Robert V. ed. *A Documentary History of Communism.* New York: Random House, 1960.

Daniels, Robert V. *The Conscience of the Revolution. Communist Opposition in Soviet Russia.* Cambridge, Massachusetts: Harvard University Press, 1960.

Daniels, Robert V., ed. *The Stalin Revolution, Fulfillment or Betrayal of Communism?* Boston: D. C. Heath and Company, 1965.

Djilas, Milovan. *The New Class, an Analysis of the Communist System.* New York: Frederick A. Praeger, 1957.

Djilas, Milovan. *The Unperfect Society, Beyond the New Class.* New York: Harcourt Brace & World, Inc., 1969.

Dodge, Peter. *A Documentary Study of Hendrik de Man, Socialist Critic of Marxism.* Princeton, New Jersey: Princeton University Press, 1979.

Fejtö, François. *A History of the People's Democracies.* New York: Praeger Publishers, 1971.

Haraszti, Miklós. *A Worker in a Worker's State.* New York: Universe Books, 1978.

Hodges, Donald C. *The Bureaucratization of Socialism.* Boston: The University of Massachusetts Press, 1981.

Kende, Péter. *Magyar füzetek* [Hungarian Pamphlets]. Budapest, Paris: Hungarian Samizdat Publishing, 1978, 1979, vol. I-IV.

Kolakowski, Leszek, ed. *The Socialist Idea: a Reappraisal.* London: Weidenfeld and Nicolson, 1974.

Kolakowski, Leszek. *Main Currents of Marxism.* Oxford: Clarendon Press, 1978, vol. I-III.

Konrád, George and Szelényi, Iván. *The Intellectuals on the Road to Class Power.* New York and London: Harcourt, Brace, Jovanovich, 1979.

Korsch, Karl. *Karl Marx.* New York: Russell & Russell, 1963.

Lenin, V. I. *The Dictatorship of the Proletariat and Elections to the Constituent Assembly.* New York: Contemporary Publishers, 1920.

Lenin, V. I. *Selected Works.* Moscow: Progress Publishers, 1967, vol. I, II, III.

Lenin, V. I. *What is Soviet Power?* Moscow: Progress Publishers, 1973.

Lenin, V. I. *Karl Marx and his Teachings.* Moscow: Progress Publishers, 1973.

Lenin, V. I. *Leninism and the World Revolutionary Working-Class Movement.* Moscow: Progress Publishers, 1976.

Lichtheim, George. *The Origins of Socialism.* New York, Washington: Frederick A. Praeger, 1969.

Lichtheim, George. *A Short History of Socialism.* New York, Washington: Praeger Publishers, 1970.

Lovell, David W. *Trotsky's Analysis of Soviet Bureaucratization.* London: Croom Helm, 1985.

de Man, Henry. *The Psychology of Socialism.* London: George Allen & Unwin Ltd., 1928.

Marcuse, Herbert. *Soviet Marxism. A Critical Analysis.* New York: Columbia University Press, 1958.

Marx, Karl and Engels, Frederick. *Selected Works.* Moscow: Foreign Languages Publishing House, 1962.

Mark, K. and Engels, F. *Manifesto of the Communist Party.* Chicago: Charles H. Kerr & Company.

Mazour, Anatole G. *Soviet Economic Development: Operation Outstrip, 1921-1965.* Princeton, New Jersey: D. Van Nostrand Company, 1967.

Medvedev, Roy A. *The Samizdat Register.* New York: W. W. Norton & Company Inc., 1977.

Medgyesy, László M. *Evolution of the Socialist "New Man" in Hungary.* Vienna: UKI, 1979.

Pellicani, Luciano. *Gramsci. An Alternative Communism?* Stanford: Hoover Institution, California, 1981.

Rizzi, Bruno. *Il Collettivismo Burocratico* [The Bureaucratic Collectivism]. Milano: Sugar Co. Edizioni, 1977.

Schumpeter, Joseph A. *Capitalism, Socialism, and Democracy.* New York: Harper & Brothers Publishers, 1950.

Sic, Ota. *The Third Way, Marxist-Leninist Theory and Modern Industrial Society.* London: Wildwood House, 1976.

Sic, Ota. *The Communist Power System.* New York: Praeger Publishers, 1981.

Sweezy, Paul M. *Marxian Socialism. Power Elite or Ruling Class.* New York: Monthly Review Press, 1956.

Sweezy, Paul M. and Battelheim, Charles. *On the Transition to Socialism.* New York and London: Monthly Review Press, 1971.

Touraine, Alaine, et al. *Solidarity, the Analysis of a Social Movement: Poland, 1980-1981.* Cambridge University Press, 1983.

Trotsky, Leon. *The Challenge of the Left Opposition (1926-27).* New York: Pathfinder Press, 1980.

Völgyes, Iván. *Political Socialization in Eastern Europe. A Comparative Framework.* New York: Praeger Publishers, 1975.

Wolter, Ulf, ed. *Rudolf Bahro, Critical Responses.* White Plains, New York: M. E. Sharpe, Inc., 1980.

INDEX

Akselrod, P. B., 4
Assessments on Marxism, 5-6
Authoritarian elements of Marxism, 10-11

Babouvist movement, 11, 103
Bahro, R., 117-118
Battelheim, C., 113-114
Bauer, R., 58
Blanc, L., 11
Bober, M. M., 17, 19
Bukharin, N. I., 94
Bureaucracy, 85, 89, 109, 116-117, 121, 128-129
Burnham, J., 6, 110

Capitalism, 125-126
Class struggle, 42
Communist Manifesto, The, 14, 21
Consciousness in socialist movement, 12, 15-16, 26, 27
Contradictions of the socialist system, 2-3

Dallin, D. J., 82-83
Daniels, R. V., 50, 56-60, 67, 74, 84
Deutscher, I., 93-94
Developmental phases in socialism, 18-19, 55
Djilas, M., 6
Dictatorship of the proletariat, 33-35, 39, 103

Eighth Congress of the Soviets, 73
End of Cold War: consequences, 1-2
Erlich, A., 66

Hilferding, R., 86-87

Industrialization, 61-62, 107
Intellectuals, 20, 30, 41, 72, 91, 95-96, 106, 108, 110-112, 118-120, 129

Kamenev, S. S., 94
Kolakowski, L., 11-12, 19, 28, 110
Kollontai, A., 71
Konrád, G., 119-120
Krassin, 91
Kronstadt Rebellion, 7, 38, 72, 74-75

Left Communists, 67
Lenin, V. I., 25, 27-28, 35, 40-41
Leninism on democracy, 38
Leninist theory on the peasantry, 36-37, 78-79, 81
Lewin, M., 81
Lichtheim, G., 12
Lutovinov, I. S., 70

Marcuse, H., 53-54, 56-57, 89-90, 92
Martov, I. O., 4
Marx, K. 12-13, 20-21, 24
Marxism, 101-102, 121-124
Medvedev, R., 96-97

Medvedev, S., 70
Moore, B., 90
More, T., 11

Nationalization and socialization, 44-46
New Economic Period (NEP), 29, 37, 64, 79, 82
Ninth Congress of the Communist Party, 70, 76

Osinsky, 70
Owen, 11

Plekhanov, G. I., 4
Political centralization, 84-85
Proudhon, P. J., 11

Rakowsky, G., 6
Rizzi, B., 109

Saint Simon, C. H., 11
Shliapnikov, A. G., 70
Sic, O., 116
Social development, 13-16, 21-23, 127-128

Socialist consciousness, 4
Socialist democracy, 104
Stalinism as Third Revolution, 49, 51, 97-99
Stalinism and voluntarism, 57-58
Statism, 16-18
Szelényi, I., 119-120
Sweezy, P., 113-117

Tomsky, M, 83
Trade Unions, 69
Transition from capitalism to socialism, 30-32
Trotsky, L., 7, 52-53, 61, 68, 70, 72, 94, 108
Tsektran, 70, 74

Unimplemented components of Marxism, 8
Unions, 72-73, 76-77

Weitling, W., 11
Wittfogel, K., 109
Workers' opposition, 71-72

Zinoviev, A., 94